Faith and Science with Dr. Fizzlebop

Brock Eastman

Faith and Science with Dr. Fizzlebop

52 fizztastically fun experiments and devotions for families

Tyndale House Publishers
Carol Stream, Illinois

Visit Tyndale online at tyndale.com.

Visit Tyndale's website for kids at tyndale.com/kids.

Visit the author online at brockeastman.com.

For manufacturing information regarding this product, please call 1-855-277-9400.

For information about special discounts for bulk purchases, please contact Tyndale House Publishers at csresponse@tyndale.com, or call 1-855-277-9400.

Library of Congress Cataloging-in-Publication Data
A catalog record for this book is available from the Library of Congress.

ISBN 978-1-4964-5816-2 (sc)

Printed in China

27	26	25	24	23	22	21
7	6	5	4	3	2	1

To my Declan (Deckie Boy):
My son, each day, I am proud to be your daddy.
You are so kind and caring to your family and friends,
always willing to help when they are in need.
And never "getfor" that you are made for wonderful things.
And as long as you wear the armor of God,
you will do wonderful things.

Contents

Introduction

Welcome to Fizzlebop Labs! I'm Dr. Phineas Einstein Fizzlebop, and I am thrilled to have your family assisting me. We're going to cover a lot of great experiments—and many of my favorite Bible stories as well.

Here at Fizzlebop Labs, my goal is to explore the amazing intricacies God programmed right into our world. And while doing so, we will learn more from the guide he gave us: the Bible.

As a scientist, I'm often questioned about how I can believe in God and trust science at the same time. But when you see how God's intricate design runs through everything, it's impossible *not* to trust God as the one behind all of it.

The Bible is full of many great stories, each teaching us something about our Creator. The experiments in this book will also teach us about how our Amazing Creator designed the world. You see, there are three things I am passionate about: God, science, and fizz!

So join me and let's grow in our knowledge of God, explore science, and make some fizz along the way. Come along as a family on this fifty-two-experiment extravaganza. Here we go!

Zealously,
Dr. P. E. Fizzlebop

P.S.—I recommend always having seltzer tablets on hand during these experiments. Because after all, everything is better with fizz. Keep your Bible near because you'll be using it with each devotional. And always wear safety goggles. Okay, let's get fizzing!

Fizzlebop Labs Experiment Preparation Notes

Each section consists of an experiment, devotional, and prayer.

We at Fizzlebop Labs suggest checking out the supply list the day prior to conducting each experiment in case you need to pick up any additional supplies. You'll also see that the Collecting Your Family's Data sections include questions about the devotional and about your observations from the experiments. So we recommend checking those out before you get started.

The **bold words** in the experiments are marvelous scientific terms. These are defined in the glossary at the back of the book.

Occasionally you'll come across a Fizz Tip, which is a way for us to help make the experiment easier or more fizztastic. You'll also see Fizz Facts along the way. These provide more insight or a wondrous fact about the experiment or devotional.

And at the end of several experiments, you'll find a FIZZ EXTRA, which directs you to another really neato experiment or swell activity on Fizzlebop.com.

We at Fizzlebop Labs believe in the Four F's: Faith, Family, Fun, and Fizz! We hope you'll share photos and videos of your experiments on social media by tagging them with #Fizzlebop. You can also write Dr. Fizzlebop a letter at 351 Executive Dr., Carol Stream, IL 60188. If we hear from you, Dr. Fizzlebop will do his very best to send you back a quick message.

Lastly, visit Fizzlebop.com to get free downloads and watch the latest Dr. Fizzlebop experiment videos.

Fizzlebop Labs Basic Equipment and Ingredient List

- Safety goggles
- Measuring cups
- Measuring spoons
- Measuring tape or ruler
- Scissors
- Permanent marker
- Water
- Baking soda
- Seltzer tablets
- Vinegar
- Food coloring
- Large glass mixing bowl
- 3 16-oz (480 mL) mason jars
- 1 16-oz (480 mL) wide-mouth mason jar
- 1 32-oz (960 mL) mason jar
- 1 32-oz (960 mL) wide-mouth mason jar
- Paper towels

CD HOVERCRAFT

The Beginning and the Spirit of God
(Genesis 1:1-2)

Introduction

Genesis 1:1-2 says, "In the beginning God created the heavens and the earth. The earth was formless and empty, and darkness covered the deep waters. And the Spirit of God was hovering over the surface of the waters." What a powerful moment.

It's the beginning of the world and the mention of a certain word that gets my imagination fizzing: *hover*.

The idea of hovering is neato. Can you imagine floating just above the ground? Well, today we're going to build a hovercraft and see how it works. And while you watch it hover, imagine the Spirit of God doing just that.

Fizzlebop Supply List

- CD or DVD (preferably one you no longer use)
- Pop-top cap from a water bottle
- Duct tape
- Balloon
- Measuring tape

The Experiment

1 Set the pop top over the center hole of the CD or DVD.

2 Use tape to secure the edges of the pop top to the disc.
FIZZ TIP: Don't leave any gaps for air to escape at the edges.

3 Push the pop-top cap closed.

4 Inflate the balloon and then twist the end (don't tie it) so the air does not escape. Stretch the opening of the balloon over the pop-top cap so that it stands directly over the disc's center.

5 Find a smooth surface for your hovercraft, then pop open the cap (while it is still inside the balloon). Give it a small tap and **observe** what happens.

6 Try filling the balloon with different amounts of air and observe what happens.
FIZZ TIP: Make it a competition! Using the same starting point each time, take turns pushing the hovercraft and measuring the distance it goes.

"Dr. Fizzlebop, what's happening?"

The air releasing from the balloon pushes down onto the surface, lifting the disc up a little bit. As the disc hovers over the pocket of air, it can easily glide without encountering **friction**. Though our hovercraft can only travel a short way, larger hovercrafts with powerful fans can move across all sorts of surfaces: rough land, snow, and even water. If your balloon was a fan producing a constant flow of air, then your hovercraft would never touch the ground.

Devotional

If you could have any superpower, what would you pick? I've always thought it'd be wondrously fizztastic to fly! So I think it's neato that the Spirit of God can hover, fly, and move freely anywhere he wants to go!

Our great, great God is a for-real, actual superhero. I'm sure you've heard of God and his Son, Jesus Christ. But you may not have heard as much about the Spirit of God. The Spirit is the most mysterious part of the Trinity (three-part God), and we often forget about him.

God the Father is patient, kind, and forgiving. Imagine a great dad who smiles a lot and has the best laugh! He zealously loves his children so much that when we do harmful or hurtful things, his heart aches and breaks for us.

The second part of God is the Son. Picture a boy with laughing eyes who's your best friend. You do everything together, can tell him anything, and know he'll never make fun of you or leave you out of things. And if you ever need help, you can call out, and he'll be the first to come running to your aid.

The third part of God is the Holy Spirit. Like I said, he's so cool because he's invisible and can move anywhere. He doesn't have a body like Jesus did on earth. Instead, the Holy Spirit—whose other name is the Holy Ghost—is an invisible being you never need to fear. Open your Bible and read Romans 8:26-27 to learn more about what the Spirit does.

Next time you feel alone, remember that you're not. If someone is mean to you, he knows it. If you cry and try to hide it, afraid you'll be made fun of, the Spirit sees your hidden tears. Better yet, he cares! And he'll pray for you with groans because you mean that much to God.

Always remember and never forget that the Father, Son, and Holy Spirit all care for you, more than you can ever imagine. The very thought makes me ecstatic!

Collecting Your Family's Data

What did your hovercraft do when you tapped it?

What did the hovercraft do when you filled the balloon with more air?

How do you feel when you think about the Spirit of God hovering near you?

What do you think the Spirit of God might groan in prayer about for you?

Prayer Time

Amazing Creator, thank you for paying attention to everything in our lives. You know when we're upset and why. Thank you that your Spirit prays for us and knows our hearts. Please teach us how to live in a way that makes you smile even more than you do now, as you keep a loving eye on each of us. Amen.

DAYTIME and NIGHTTIME

Light and Dark

(Genesis 1:3-5, 14-19)

Introduction

Could you imagine what it would be like if there was no sun? If the sky was always cold and dark? Well, at the very beginning of time, that's how it was, at least until God spoke. He said, "Let there be light." And you know what? There was light. A short time later—the fourth day, in fact—he made the sun, the stars, and the moon. Stupendous!

Now imagine if there was no night. I for one would have a very tough time sleeping, even if my dinosaur curtains were pulled tight. But thankfully God did create both day and night. He made a perfect system to keep our surroundings lit and warm sometimes, and cool and dark at other times. Today we're going to learn about how the Earth's rotation causes day and night.

FIZZ FACT: Did you know that there are days where the sun never sets in places like Finland, Sweden, Canada, Russia, Norway, and Iceland, as well as Alaska in the United States? These places also experience days of total darkness, where the sun never rises.

Fizzlebop Supply List

- Masking tape
- Large ball (soccer or basketball works best)
- Permanent marker
- Flashlight
- Dark room
- 2 family members or friends
- Small ball (tennis or baseball works best)

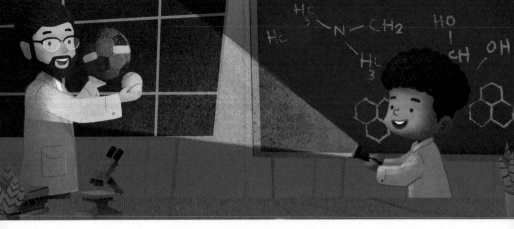

The Experiment

1. Cut 4 1-inch (2.5 cm) pieces of tape.

2. Space the pieces of tape equally around the large ball. If this were a globe, you'd be putting the tape around the equator.

3. Write *A* on one piece of tape, *B* on another, *C* on another, and *D* on the last piece. These will be our coordinates.

4. Place the underside of the ball on your palm. This ball represents the Earth.

5. While leaving the flashlight off, have one person aim it at the ball and be ready to turn it on. The flashlight represents the sun.

6. Have the other person turn off the lights in the room.

7. Now the person holding the flashlight should say, "Let there be light," and turn on the flashlight.

Rotate the ball left to right (counterclockwise) so a different letter is now in the brightness of the flashlight. Note what is happening to each piece of tape as you rotate the ball. Is it moving into darkness? Into light?

While still holding the large ball (Earth), pick up the small ball, which represents the moon, in your other hand. Keep the flashlight pointed at the same spot on the Earth and move the moon counterclockwise in a circle around the Earth. Note the shadows cast by each ball. Are they the same size?

"Dr. Fizzlebop, what's happening?"

What I like most about this experiment is that we get to see it play out every day. Every 24 hours, the Earth rotates (which is another way to say "spins"). The location you're at moves away from the sun and goes from day, to dusk, to night. But the Earth continues to rotate, so night turns to dawn, and then day. The sun itself never dims. When we brought the small ball into the experiment, we saw Earth's shadow cast upon it.

To learn more about the moon, check out a yummy FIZZ EXTRA below.

Devotional

The sun is really an amazing thing, and so is the Earth. But even more amazing is how they are perfectly positioned in our solar system. The Earth is the right distance from the sun to make life possible, and its precise rotation causes day and night to happen. The moon revolves around the Earth, creating tides in our oceans. It really is an ideal system, and one only a creative God could have put into action. We'll learn more about God's design for us and our world as we do more experiments and devotions together.

For now, though, open your Bible and read Genesis 1:3-5 and 1:14-19. God knew exactly what he was doing when he created the universe!

Tomorrow, set your alarm for a few minutes before sunrise (and ask your family to do the same!). When you wake up, step outside and find a spot where you can glimpse the rising sun. Close your eyes and let its warmth wash over you. Can you see the glow, even with your eyes closed? The rising and setting sun is a reminder to me that God makes each day new, that his plan is perfect and always works. That warmth you feel, that glow you see, will always be there—just as God will always be there for you.

Collecting Your Family's Data

Which coordinates (letters) on the globe are in the light at the beginning of the experiment?

Which coordinates were lit when you rotated the globe?

Does the moon become darker when you move it to certain locations?

Describe the feeling of the sun's warmth on your face.

How does it feel to know God will always be there for you?

Prayer Time

Amazing Creator, we're grateful that you created a time for us to be awake and to enjoy the beautiful world you created. And we are thankful for a time of darkness when we can close our eyes and sleep. May we rest knowing that with the morning sun, each day is new, and with the setting sun, we can go to bed putting our trust in you. Amen.

FIZZ EXTRA: Phases of the Moon

The moon is a marvelous orb floating up in space. You know now that the moon doesn't create its own light. Instead, it reflects the light of the sun. The moon looks different depending on its position and the location of the sun. That's how we have different phases of the moon. Astronomers (who are scientists that study everything in the universe beyond Earth's atmosphere) even have names for when the moon looks different, including supermoon, blood moon, blue moon, harvest moon, and more. Have you ever seen one of these special moon phases?

Create your own phases of the moon with this very yummy **FIZZ EXTRA** and discover what each phase looks like.

Find the **PHASES OF THE MOON** project at Fizzlebop.com, or scan this QR code and click or tap **FIZZ EXTRA**.

GROWING a GARDEN

The Garden of Eden
(Genesis 2:8-9)

Introduction

When I think of a garden, I envision my favorite vegetables, fruits, and herbs, like juicy red tomatoes, fresh cilantro, and especially crisp green broccoli. I also picture my mom's butterfly garden full of coneflowers, lavender, and lantanas. Have you ever wondered what the Garden of Eden was like? I imagine God's creativity in full bloom, from fruit trees to fragrant flowers to lush ferns. I imagine lying on the thick branch of a kapok tree and reading a book. Well, of course there weren't books in the Garden of Eden, but still I can dream of it. Each plant in the garden was specially designed, and each had a purpose—which is also true of the plants in today's world. That leads me to today's experiment. We're going to observe how plants grow and how God made each one unique from the very start.

Fizzlebop Supply List

- Permanent marker
- 3 16-oz (480 mL) mason jars
- 3 paper towels
- 1/2 cup (120 mL) water
- 3 types of seeds: pea, green bean, and sunflower

FIZZ TIP: You may use other seeds too—these are just suggestions.

The Experiment

Mark each jar with the type of seed you will be planting in it.

FIZZ TIP: You can write directly on glass jars with a permanent marker and easily wash it off when you're done.

Dampen the paper towels. Fold them in half and push each one into a jar.

FIZZ TIP: Be careful not to soak the paper towels.

Carefully push seeds down into the paper towels along the wall of the jar so the seeds are secure. Seeds should be visible through the glass. After all, we need to see them to observe them.

Place the jar somewhere warm, like a windowsill. Sunlight is important, but avoid too much direct sunlight.

5 Keep the paper towels damp by putting a little water on them every day.

6 Over the next week, observe the jars and record your findings in the observation spaces below.

"Dr. Fizzlebop, what's happening?"

After about a week of watering and sunlight, your seedlings should be sprouting and growing. **Germination** is the development of a plant from a seed that has been dormant (which is like sleeping). Seedlings require the right conditions to successfully grow from a seed. Two key ingredients are water and oxygen. Many seeds germinate when the temperature is slightly above normal room temperature. Yet other seeds need warmer temperatures, cooler temperatures, or even temperature **fluctuations** (which means changes). While light is often an important trigger for germination, some seeds instead need darkness to germinate.

Devotional

"Then God said, 'Let the land sprout with vegetation—every sort of seed-bearing plant, and trees that grow seed-bearing fruit. These seeds will then produce the kinds of plants and trees from which they came.' And that is what happened. The land produced vegetation—all sorts of seed-bearing plants, and trees with seed-bearing fruit. Their seeds produced plants and trees of the same kind. And God saw that it was good" (Genesis 1:11-12).

In the very beginning of the Bible (Genesis 1:11-12), we read about how God created plants. You see, when God unveiled his creation, he knew the design and intricacies of every living thing. He had a plan for them not only to grow but to produce more of their own kind. To do that, he put a genetic blueprint inside each seed, telling it how to grow and become the very best plant of its kind it could be.

God's design for our world didn't stop at plants. He created animals, he designed the seasons, and he formed you, uniquely and specially. And as you grow, you get to experience a plan designed to make you *you*, just as God saw you before you were born. Now that's magnificent.

So look at the members of your family. What traits do you see? Are there similarities between you and your parents, siblings, grandparents, or cousins? What differences do you notice? Even if you're an identical twin or triplet and look the same as your siblings, God still created you uniquely.

Like the plants in this experiment, you need oxygen and water, but you also need to dig deep into the Word of God and grow in your relationship with him to discover the blueprint he designed for you. And though I don't know God's plans for me, I know they are good, because he says in Romans 8:28, "We know that God causes everything to work together for the good of those who love God and are called according to his purpose for them."

Collecting Your Family's Data

Record the progress of each seed below.

Day 3 Observations:
Seed 1:

Seed 2:

Seed 3:

Day 6 Observations:
Seed 1:

....

Seed 2:

....

Seed 3:

....

If you used other kinds of seeds for your experiment, we'd love to hear how they did! Share your results with us at Fizzlebop.com.

Which seed sprouted first?

....

Which seed had the longest sprout (most growth) on day 3?

....

Which seed had the longest sprout (most growth) on day 6?

....

In what ways are you unique compared to the rest of your family?

....

Where do you believe God is leading you (career, places, dreams)?

....

Prayer Time

Thank the Amazing Creator for the world around you, for the plants, animals, sun, and rain. Do you have a favorite animal or flower or fruit? Thank God for that specifically when you pray. He's the Creator of this wondrous world we get to live in and care for, and he loves it when we talk to him about his creation.

RAIN CLOUDS

Noah's Ark
(Genesis 6:9–7:24)

Introduction

Greetings! I'm glad to see you today. I was just reading one of my favorite Bible stories: Noah's ark. I'm always struck by how God used rain clouds to bring rain and flood the earth, then a rainbow to signal the end of the flood. Rain clouds, rain, rainbow. I think that's called alliteration. I'm more of a science guy than a grammar guy, but sometimes I surprise myself. Anyhow . . .

We're going to learn about rain clouds and rain in this experiment, and our next experiment will focus on rainbows. Best of all, we'll get to spend double the time with the faithful Noah and his family—and that wondrous engineering marvel, the ark.

Fizzlebop Supply List

- 16-oz (480 mL) mason jar
- 1 1/2 cups (360 mL) water
- Can of shaving cream (white)
- Food coloring (at least three colors)
- An eyedropper or pipette if your food coloring is no squeezable

The Experiment

Pour the water into the jar.

Squirt shaving cream on top of the water in a light layer, covering the surface completely.

Let the shaving cream cloud **expand** and stiffen like a billowing thunderhead.

Next, choose your first color of food coloring and squirt several droplets in the same location on the cloud.

Repeat this with a few more colors at different points on the cloud's top surface.

Observe as the colorful downpour begins inside your container.

"Dr. Fizzlebop, what's happening?"

The shaving cream cloud is light and airy like a real cloud (low **density**), but when you add the food coloring droplets (higher density), you're adding extra weight the cloud can't hold. The color droplets fall to the bottom of the cloud and pour out like rain.

Devotional

Remember how your shaving cream cloud expanded bigger and bigger at first? Can you imagine if a rain cloud grew and grew and grew? And then it started to rain and rain and rain? So much rain that it filled the entire world? That's the beginning of the story of Noah, a story with a lot of rain and a really big ark.

And we'll get back to that ark in a moment, but first, take a few minutes and read Genesis 6:9–7:24.

In the story, everyone in the world was rejecting God. Everyone except Noah and his family: they had faith, and they still worshiped God. Because of this, God entrusted Noah with an extraordinary task: to start the world over again. Not only did God entrust Noah, but Noah had to trust God. Though everyone mocked Noah and his family for following God's plan to build a massive ark, Noah believed what God had told him, and his family was saved.

There will be moments in your life where following God's teaching will be difficult, or maybe it won't seem to make sense. Studying science reminds me of the truth of who God is. I see the intricacy of his design when I look at a cell under a microscope or observe a honeybee as it flies from flower to flower. And I know he will never let me down because God is always working in the lives of those who trust him.

Trusting God is just the beginning of the story—both yours, mine, and Noah's.

And remember—we have a second Noah-related experiment coming up! Because what do you get when the sun comes out after the rain? A rainbow.

Collecting Your Family's Data

What did you notice about the pattern of your rainfall?

....

With what task did God trust Noah?

....

Have you had to trust God with something complicated or almost unbelievable? If yes, what was it?

....

Prayer Time

Take a moment and talk about a time when your family had to make a big decision, perhaps one that seemed in opposition to what the world around you said was right. Praise God for giving your family the courage and strength needed for that decision.

FIZZ EXTRA: Popsicle Stick Boat

The ark was a marvelous feat of engineering at a time when something of such enormous size might have been unimaginable, especially considering the tools available and the small number of people working on the project. Building the ark was a wonderful example of Noah's trust in God. Noah was being asked to build a boat on dry land in preparation for a flood unlike anything the world had ever seen. Yet he did. I wonder, would I? Would you?

Take on this FIZZ EXTRA and build your very own Popsicle stick boat. I've even laid out three levels of difficulty for your family to try. And when you're done, see which constructions work best on the open water (a pond or pool) and which are best for moving water (a stream).

Find the POPSICLE STICK BOAT project at Fizzlebop.com, or scan this QR code and click or tap FIZZ EXTRA.

MELTED CRAYON RAINBOW

God's Covenant with Noah
(Genesis 9:12-17)

Introduction

I'm ecstatic you've come back for part two of our Noah experiments! Today we're going to look at one of God's most colorful creations: rainbows. And you won't have to wait for a storm to pass to see this one. We'll be using crayons and heat to recreate a rainbow with this magnificent experiment, and we'll also learn the significance of the rainbow in Noah's story.

WARNING! This experiment requires high heat. Safety first! And like many of our experiments, it can be messy, so make sure to protect the area you are working in.

Fizzlebop Supply List

- Crayons (red, orange, yellow, green, blue, violet, and indigo if you have it)
- Double-sided piece of tape
- Piece of white letter-size (or A4 size) cardstock
- Easel (or a few books will do the trick)
- Pair of safety goggles for each person
- Hair dryer

The Experiment

1. Peel the paper off each crayon.

2. Line up the crayons in the color order of a real rainbow.

3. Tape the crayons to the top center of the cardstock.

4. Attach the cardstock to the easel or lean it against a stack of books.

   FIZZ TIP: Place some paper towels under the bottom of the cardstock for easier cleanup.

5. Put on your safety goggles.

6. Aim the hair dryer at the bottom tips of the crayons and turn the hair dryer on high.

7. Observe as the solid wax of the crayons melts and liquefies, then begins to stream down the cardstock.

8. Do not touch the melted crayons until they have had time to cool.

"Dr. Fizzlebop, what's happening?"

Crayons are made of wax, and wax happens to be a marvelous substance. It can go from solid to liquid and back to solid, all with a change in temperature. When you applied the heat from the hair dryer to the crayons, they liquefied, and the hot wax dripped down the cardstock. And when you stopped using the hair dryer, the wax began to cool and re-form into a solid. This is called a reversible physical change, and you saw it in true wondrous color.

Devotional

Now that you've **replicated** a rainbow, let's go more in-depth to understand the significance (which means importance) of this colorful display of beauty. First, open your Bible and read the next part of Noah's story in Genesis 8 and 9.

Talk about patience! Noah built a gigantic boat in the middle of the desert, trusting that God would bring rain. After everything was flooded (for 150 days!), Noah and his family and all the animals were stuck in the boat together, hoping and believing that God would keep his promise. Noah didn't know when he would step foot on dry land again. All he had was the faith that God would come through as he had in the past.

And he did!

Noah and his family finally made it to dry ground, and God provided a symbol of promise: a colorful rainbow. This beautiful colorful bow through the sky exemplifies God's faithfulness. What a magnificent and exuberant way to display his commitment to the covenant he made with his people. And he promised that from then on, the rainbow following the rain would be a reminder to him of this covenant.

God wants us to put our trust in him, remember his faithfulness, and trust his words like Noah did. A few years back, I had a tough decision to make. Should I continue working for the university? I had a good salary, health insurance, and all that important adult stuff there—but I couldn't openly discuss my work through a biblical lens. Or should I start my very own lab? The university wasn't asking me not to be a Christian, but they didn't want me mentioning God in my scientific papers anymore. I'd asked my fellow scientists, my parents, and even my cat, Snickerdoodle, what the best choice was, but even with their answers, I was unsure. As I prayed about it one morning, I felt God was leading me toward one choice over the other. That afternoon, I made my decision in faith. Not an hour later, as a rainstorm passed over, a double rainbow spread across the dark sky. And without a doubt, I knew God was confirming my decision to open Fizzlebop Labs. Have you ever had an experience like that?

Next time you see a rainbow, be reminded of what God has already done in your life. The rainbow is a gift, a symbol of God's promise to those who love and trust him.

FIZZ TIP: Hang your crayon rainbow somewhere in your house for all to see—and as a reminder of God's promise to you.

Collecting Your Family's Data

Observe how the wax dripped down the cardstock. What could you have done to change the flow of the melted wax?

....

Can you think of other substances that can undergo reversible change? I'll give you a hint: one can go on toast. Another, every human needs.

....

Write down something amazing God has done in your life.

....

Write down something you need to trust God with today.

....

Prayer Time

Take a moment as a family to thank God for the amazing things he has done in your life. Then ask God to help you with the things you still need to trust him with.

NINE-LEVEL DENSITY TOWER

Tower of Babel
(Genesis 11:1-9)

Introduction

As a kid, I attended a lot of family get-togethers, and those gatherings sometimes had a hundred people or more. The best part was always my Great-Aunt Lois's seven-layer Jell-O salad. But at a party that big, it was really important to communicate when it was time for dessert. Have you ever walked up to a dessert table and found that your favorite seven-layer Jell-O salad is gone? Well, I have. You're not going to want to eat today's marvelous masterpiece of liquid layers, but it will look swell when we're finished. And we'll learn a thing or two about communication along the way.

Fizzlebop Supply List

- Clear half-gallon (2 L) pitcher or vase
- Turkey baster
- 9 containers for separating liquids
- 1 cup (240 mL) honey
- 1 cup (240 mL) light corn syrup
- 1 cup (240 mL) maple syrup
- 1 cup (240 mL) whole milk
- 1 cup (240 mL) dish soap
- 1 cup (240 mL) water
- 1 cup (240 mL) vegetable oil
- 1 cup (240 mL) rubbing alcohol
- 1 cup (240 mL) lamp oil
- Red and green food coloring (or blue food coloring—see Fizz Tip below)
- Metal bolt
- Popcorn kernels

The Experiment

1. Pour each liquid into one of the 9 containers. Either label each cup or set them in the order you'll add them to the larger container: honey, corn syrup, maple syrup, whole milk, dish soap, water, vegetable oil, rubbing alcohol, and lamp oil.

2. Add 5 drops of red food coloring to the water and 5 drops of green food coloring to the rubbing alcohol for contrast so they stand out in the finished column.

   FIZZ TIP: If your dish soap is green, consider adding blue food coloring to the rubbing alcohol instead.

3. Start building your tower by pouring the honey into the clear container. It's important to *slowly* layer the honey, corn syrup, and maple syrup into the center of your container. Be sure the liquids don't touch the sides of the container as you pour.

- Game dice
- Cherry tomato
- Plastic beads
- Soda bottle cap
- Ping-Pong ball
- Seltzer tablet (because everything is better with fizz)

29

4 Using the turkey baster, carefully add the milk, followed by the dish soap. Add them just a little at a time.

FIZZ TIP: Slowly and carefully is the best way to successfully complete this experiment.

5 This time we're going to use the side of the container. Fill the turkey baster with the water, then hold the tip of the baster against the side of the container and close to the layer of dish soap. Now squeeze gently, allowing the water to flow down the inside wall of the container.

6 Layer the vegetable oil, the rubbing alcohol, and the lamp oil with the same method. Step back and observe your nine-level density tower as the liquids settle and separate.

7 Release the objects one at a time into the liquids, allowing them to fall as gently as possible through the density levels. Start with the bolt, followed by the popcorn kernels, the game dice, the cherry tomato, the plastic beads, the **soda** bottle cap, and lastly the Ping-Pong ball.

FIZZ TIP: Release the objects at different locations around the container and allow the top levels of the tower to settle between each release. A few of the objects may have odd effects on your tower. Observe and note in the spaces below.

8 Once you have observed and enjoyed your tower, grab a seltzer tablet and set it on the top layer. Observe the fizzy destruction.

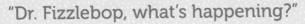

"Dr. Fizzlebop, what's happening?"

The tower you created put density differences on display. Basically, density is how much "substance" is packed into a particular volume. Each liquid you added has a different density, and those with the highest densities sit at the lowest levels of the tower. Density differences also apply to the objects you dropped into the tower. The densest objects sank to the bottom, and the least dense floated on top.

Devotional

Communication is a critical skill for anyone to have. It allows us to share our ideas and needs, to seek information, to record our history, and to achieve goals. But communication can also cause problems.

Open your Bible and read Genesis 11:1-9.

This is an interesting chapter in our biblical history. It follows the Great Flood and God's command for his people to go forth and multiply, yet once again God's people disobeyed him. Instead they found a valley and settled there. They wanted to establish a great city and build a tower that reached into the sky. They sought fame and wished not to be scattered all over the earth, yet God had just told them to spread out across the world.

In direct defiance to his command, they settled and, brick by brick, began building a tall tower. The people wished to make a monument to their own greatness. They hoped to establish a powerful city to honor themselves, not God. But God ended this misguided notion that they could be greater than him by disrupting their communication.

If you want to communicate well, it's important to speak clearly and listen carefully so the "layers" of meaning aren't disturbed or distorted. When you dropped the fizz tablet into the nine-level density tower, it caused a huge disruption. The liquids began churning and swirling and rising and falling, making a rather unorganized mess—nothing like the beauty of your original layered tower.

That's what God did to the people who tried to build the tower of Babel. He gave them different languages to disrupt their ability to communicate and to end the project. It worked. The tower was never finished, and the people began to spread across the earth.

Collecting Your Family's Data

What did you observe as you added the different liquids to your density tower?

....

Which objects floated, and which liquids did they float in?

....

Why did God disrupt the communication of the people building the tower of Babel?

....

How might you help improve your family's communication? For example, try thinking of ways you could be a good listener to your family members.

....

Prayer Time

As a family, pray for God to strengthen your communication with each other, through kind words, and engaging deeply in each other's hopes, desires, and dreams. Ask God how you can communicate his message to your neighbors and the community around you.

FIZZ EXTRA: Liquid Weights

Want to go deeper with this experiment? You can weigh each liquid on a kitchen scale. Be sure the volumes are all the same, of course—so perhaps compare 1 cup (240 mL) of water to 1 cup (240 mL) of honey. Which is heavier? Which is lower in the density tower? It should be the heavier of the two liquids.

SPARKLY CRYSTAL CREATIONS

Pillar of Salt
(Genesis 19:26)

Introduction

In this experiment, we're going to grow something that isn't alive. Sounds kind of cool. Now, this isn't like the novel *Frankenstein*, though indeed that is a marvelous novel. Instead, we're going to use a **chemical reaction** to grow a **crystal**. To do this, we need to follow the instructions carefully. When we don't obey the instructions—in experiments or in other parts of life—the consequences can be catastrophic! So pay close attention to each and every step.

WARNING! This experiment requires hot water, scissors, and borax. Safety first! Do not ingest borax.

Fizzlebop Supply List

- Wide-mouth 32-oz (960 mL) mason jar
- Several pipe cleaners
- Ball of string
- Scissors
- Pencil
- Tape
- 3 cups (720 mL) water
- 18 tbsp (270 grams) borax
- Food coloring
- Spoon
- Drinking glass
- Spool of ribbon

34

The Experiment

1 Get creative. Twist pipe cleaners into a design of your choosing, like a star or a heart. This will become your ornament.

FIZZ TIP: Make sure the pipe cleaner shape will fit through the mouth of the jar with extra space on either side.

2 Cut about 3 inches (7.5 cm) of string. Tie one end of the string to the pipe cleaner shape and tie the other end around the middle of a pencil.

3 Lower the pipe cleaner shape into the jar with the pencil resting across the mouth of the jar to make sure the string isn't too long. Then take the pipe cleaner shape out of the jar and set it aside.

FIZZ TIP: Your pipe cleaner shape should not touch any part of the jar. If it touches the bottom, then roll the pencil so that the string shortens. Apply a piece of tape to where the string wraps around the pencil to hold it in place.

4 Pour the water into the jar and microwave the jar for 3 to 5 minutes or until it begins to **boil**.

WARNING! The water will be hot, so carefully remove the jar from the microwave using hot pads, and set it on a heat-safe surface. Do not put the pipe cleaner in the microwave.

5 Add the borax to the jar.

6 Add 5 to 10 drops of your choice of food coloring to the jar.

7 Stir the borax and food coloring into the water with a spoon so it **dissolves** as much as possible. You should still see some particles of borax floating in the water.

FIZZ TIP: If you do not see any particles of borax floating, add another tablespoon and stir. You want a well-saturated **solution**.

8 Lower the pipe cleaner shape into the jar so it is completely covered with the borax-water solution.

9 Let your pipe cleaner shape sit overnight.

10 In the morning, gently remove the crystal-covered pipe cleaner shape (your ornament), and let it dry by hanging it in an empty drinking glass (or an empty jar if your drinking glasses are too narrow).

11 Once the crystals are completely dry, cut off the string and tie a ribbon to the top of the ornament. You can now hang the ornament on your tree at Christmastime or near a window—or give it as a gift!

"Dr. Fizzlebop, what's happening?"

Borax is a chemical that forms crystals under the right conditions. You first created a **saturated** chemical solution by mixing the boiling water and borax together. When you inserted your pipe cleaner shape into the solution, you gave the borax particles something to attach to. That's when the crystals began to form, which in turn allowed more and more layers of crystals to form on top of each other as the temperature of your solution continued to cool. **Evaporation** of the water caused additional borax to crystallize on the pipe cleaner.

Devotional

Whew! That was an awfully nifty neato experiment! But I do have one fizzy confession to make about our little science project. Okay. Ready for it? Here it is: the first time I tried this project, I actually didn't follow the directions. Instead of watching crystals form on my pipe cleaner, I spilled everything in a fizzy-dizzy mess all over the counter. Food coloring, pipe cleaners, and water were everywhere.

When we don't follow the instructions—whether we're doing science experiments or baking my favorite super-simple triple chocolate chunk caramel cookies—we end up not getting the results we want.

There's a story in the Bible about someone who didn't follow directions. And it was a disaster for sure. Here's what happened: this guy named Lot was living in a city called Sodom, where there was a lot of bad stuff going on. In fact, things were so bad, God decided to destroy the city. But anyone who followed God would be able to escape.

Only Lot and his family followed God, so God sent two angels to warn them to get out of Sodom as fast as they could! But the angels gave them a warning: "Run for your lives! And don't look back or stop anywhere in the valley! Escape to the mountains, or you'll be swept away!"

So Lot, his wife, and his daughters ran out of the city. But as they were running away, Lot's wife glanced back to see what was happening. At the moment she turned around to look, she turned into a pillar of salt.

Yikes. Lot's wife didn't follow the directions, and it ended up in a big mess.

Later in the Bible, Jesus gave us two really important directions to follow in life. Grab your Bible and look up Mark 12:29-31. See if you can figure out what the two directions are that God gave us!

If you guessed loving God and loving others, then you got it! When we love God and other people, we'll see how the love of God changes everything—just like how borax changed into crystals on the pipe cleaner, creating something brand new and wondrous!

Collecting Your Family's Data

How quickly did you notice crystals beginning to form?

....

Did your pipe cleaner design work well for growing crystals? What would you do differently next time?

....

Think of a time you were given instructions from someone you trusted, but you didn't listen to them. What happened?

....

Prayer Time

Magnificent Son, help us to love you and love others. We know that when we follow those two simple directions, we'll start to see wondrous changes in our lives and in the lives of people around us! Thank you, Jesus, for showing us the way to love God and love others! Amen.

FIZZ EXTRA: Tasty Treat

Did you know science can be yummy too? Well, baking *is* science: we mix ingredients together to create something new. Today we have a very special recipe, created by our very own Chef Deliciopop.

Bake your own Super-Simple Triple Chocolate Chunk Caramel Cookies with this very yummy FIZZ EXTRA and discover the science of baking.

Find the TASTY TREAT recipe at Fizzlebop.com, or scan this QR code and click or tap FIZZ EXTRA.

WALKING RAINBOW

Joseph and the Coat of Many Colors
(Genesis 37)

Introduction

Simple yet extravagant, this experiment is marvelously colorful. And, you know, it reminds me of a Bible story about something that was also marvelously colorful: Joseph's coat of many colors. Today you'll watch as color walks up white sheets of paper towel and becomes a stupendous display. We at Fizzlebop Labs call it the Walking Rainbow.

Fizzlebop Supply List

- 7 clear 8-oz (240 mL) glasses or plastic cups
- 4 cups (960 mL) water
- Food coloring (red, yellow, and blue)
- Roll of paper towels
- Scissors

FIZZ TIP: Paper towels that divide into half sheets and are highly **absorbent** work best.

The Experiment

1 Put all 7 clear cups in a row and fill the first, third, fifth, and seventh cups nearly to the top with water. Leave the others empty.

2 Add 10 drops of red food coloring to the first cup and the seventh cup.

3 Add 10 drops of yellow food coloring to the third cup.

4 Add 10 drops of blue food coloring to the fifth cup.

5 Rip 6 half sheets of paper towel from your roll. (If you have regular-size paper towels, rip off 3 sheets and cut them in half lengthwise.)

6 Fold each half sheet of paper towel in half lengthwise and in half again lengthwise.

7 Trim the paper towel sheets so they are about 8 inches (20 cm) long. Make sure the ends of the paper towels can reach the bottoms of each cup, from one cup to the cup next to it. If you use taller glasses, you may need to leave the paper towels full-length.

8 Place one end of your folded paper towel in the first cup and place the other end in the second cup. Then do the same with another paper towel from the second cup into the third cup. Continue this process (third cup to fourth, fourth to fifth, fifth to sixth) for all seven cups.

9 Observe what happens.

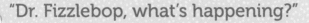

"Dr. Fizzlebop, what's happening?"

While you should immediately see the colored water absorbed into the paper towels, what happens in the empty cups is the wondrous part. Check back every couple of minutes, and soon you will notice that the colored water has walked up each paper towel and is starting to walk down into the neighboring empty cup. A little longer and those empty cups will fill with colored water, and by the end of the experiment, all of the cups will end up with the same amount of water in them. Since the empty cups start with a different color on either side, the colors will blend together. Eventually you should see three new colors added to your lineup of cups. You have officially made a walking rainbow!

Devotional

I don't know about you, but when we tried this experiment at Fizzlebop Labs, we had wide eyes and open mouths! God's wondrous world is truly magnificent. God is so creative, and I just love all the colors he thought up!

Have you ever tried to come up with a new color before? It's a real brain-buster!

Colors are all around us, and there's a story in the Bible all about a colorful object. Take a minute and open up your Bible to Genesis 37.

Joseph was one of the twelve sons of Jacob, and Jacob gave him something very special: a colorful robe. That robe was definitely a fizztastic gift. But even though Joseph really liked the robe, his brothers were jealous instead of ecstatic for him.

Have you ever been jealous before? Jealousy is when you look at something someone else has and you wish you had it instead of them. God actually warned us about jealousy. In Exodus 20:17, God said: "You must not covet [or be jealous of!] your neighbor's house . . . or anything else that belongs to your neighbor."

But why would God warn us about jealousy? Well, jealousy is super sneaky. It starts like a little bit of color traveling through a paper towel until it reaches the other side, and suddenly you see jealousy everywhere! One minute you're doing swell, and the next minute you're feeling like nothing will be marvelous again until you have what belongs to someone else.

One time I got super jealous. It happened when I entered this huge science experiment competition. Each scientist was supposed to create his or her own special experiment, and then the judges would decide which one was the most magnificent. Well, my experiment went well, but my friend Dr. Swishpop had an experiment that honestly was better than mine. Her experiment was stupendous! But . . . I let jealousy get in the way.

And instead of being excited for my friend, I was jealous. In fact, I didn't talk to her the whole rest of the competition. But later I stopped and remembered this very story about Joseph and his brothers who were jealous. And so I went and congratulated Dr. Swishpop and asked God for forgiveness for my jealousy.

If you're feeling jealous of someone else, take a second and thank God for that person. Thank God for the gift that he gave to them. And then thank God for the gifts and good things he's given *you*. You might be surprised at how many good things God has done for you that you can be thankful for!

Collecting Your Family's Data

What new colors did you see created?

....

Did any of the colors "walk" more quickly than the others?

....

Think of a time you were jealous of someone. How did you handle your jealousy?

....

Prayer Time

Amazing Creator, forgive us when we feel jealous of other people. Help us to be excited for them and help us to be thankful for all the good things you've done for us. Thank you for being a wondrous God who does wondrous things! Amen.

BENDING WATER with STATIC ELECTRICITY

Crossing the Red Sea
(Exodus 14)

Introduction

Did you know that water can bend? Well, sure, you've seen it flow around a curve in a river, and you can imagine it curving and turning in the pipes in your house. But we're going to actually make it bend in midair while it's flowing freely from your faucet—no pipes or muddy riverbanks required. Plus, you'll only need a couple of items to make it happen. I'm ec-*static* for you to try this super-simple experiment.

Fizzlebop Supply List

- Inflated balloon
- Narrow stream of water from a faucet

The Experiment

1. Turn on the water and allow a very narrow stream to flow into the sink.

2. Rub your hair with the balloon a dozen times.

3. Slowly move the balloon toward the stream of water (but don't let the balloon touch the water).

4. Watch closely and observe what happens.

"Dr. Fizzlebop, what's happening?"

While rubbing the balloon against your hair, **static electricity** began to build on the balloon. The stream of water is attracted to the built-up static electricity. As the balloon nears the water, the stream begins to bend! But why?

As you rub your hair with the balloon, **electrons** (negatively charged particles) jump from your hair to the balloon as they rub together. The balloon is now negatively charged because it has gained more electrons. Water **molecules** have a positive end and a negative end, so they are electrically neutral. When you move the negatively charged balloon toward the water, the positive ends of the water molecules are attracted toward the negatively charged balloon. That causes the stream of water to bend. The bending stops when the balloon repels the negative ends of the water molecules, preventing the water from touching the balloon. Neato!

Devotional

In this experiment, you bent a small stream of water with static electricity. In the Bible, God did something way more incredible: he split apart an entire sea.

Take a few minutes to read the story in Exodus 14.

When God's people were in a tight spot, he told Moses to lift his staff over the Red Sea, and that night God sent a strong wind to blow the water back until there was a dry path for the Israelite people to walk safely across. The water literally bent in different directions, like our experiment times a gazillion. Magnificent!

You know, in my life there have been times when I felt stuck. Once, when I was in third grade, I had an important geology test after lunch. I was so nervous I didn't even open my Astro Dinosaur Explorer lunch box. I couldn't remember anything because I was panicking so much—What type of rock is created by lava? What's the name of the layer just below the Earth's crust? And so forth.

So you know what I did? I remembered to stop and be still. And then I talked to God about my situation. I asked for God's help to be calm and focus. And what do you know? When the test came, God gave me peace and helped me do my best after all the hours of studying I had put in.

God wants to help us when we're feeling stuck. Next time you're worried about a test, a disagreement with a friend, a sick family member, or anything else, take a moment to stop and tell God all about it. God wants to hear from us every day. And God is never too busy to listen. So what are you waiting for? Stop right now and tell God about something that's making you worry or panic.

Collecting Your Family's Data

What happened when you put the balloon near the water?

....

We used a balloon and the power of static electricity to bend our water. What did God use to hold the Red Sea back?

....

What's something you could ask for God's help with today?

....

Prayer Time

Share your worries with your family and ask them what they're worried about right now. Take some time to pray for each other. Ask our Amazing Creator to give your family peace as you all face what comes next.

THE POWER of SOUND WAVES

The Walls of Jericho
(Joshua 6)

Introduction

The sky is gray, the rain is pattering outside, and suddenly your house shakes with the rumble of thunder. Or maybe you're at a concert where you can feel the deep beat of the drum or low strum of the bass guitar. When the Israelites marched around the city of Jericho in the Bible, they blew their horns as loud as they could, and they kept this up for several days. Sound is an invisible force that can have visible effects, and we're going to see those effects in today's experiment. That's right, we're going to *see* sound!

Fizzlebop Supply List

- Wide-mouth 16-oz (480 mL) mason jar
- Plastic wrap
- Large rubber band
- Sea salt crystals

The Experiment

1. Stretch a piece of plastic wrap over the top of the mason jar so it's **taut** (which means tight).

2. Secure the plastic to the jar with a large rubber band. Be sure that the plastic wrap is tight and does not sag.

3. Sprinkle salt crystals in the middle of the plastic wrap.

4. Get close to the salt crystals and speak loudly! What happens?

5. Experiment with shouting and whispering. Observe what happens when you sing instead of talk.

"Dr. Fizzlebop, what's happening?"

While you might think it's your breath making the salt crystals jump and move, it's actually the sound **vibrations**. Sound travels in waves, and these waves cause the plastic wrap surface to vibrate, which then causes the crystals to bounce or shiver. If you have a stereo or sub-woofer in your house, place the jar on the floor near it. Then turn on some music and observe what the music does to the crystals at different volumes. Sound may be an invisible force, but it is powerful and can have visible effects on its surroundings. Isn't that magnificent?

Devotional

Have you ever been surprised when you heard a sound you weren't expecting? You might have jumped like the sea salt crystals on the plastic wrap. I know I have. One time, one of my experiments was quietly bubbling and fizzing. It was a most melodic symphony. Then, all of a sudden, a *BOOM* blasted from the beaker. I leapt onto the lab table like when my cat, Snickerdoodle, saw a cucumber for the first time. A second later, my experiment was oozing and foaming all over the floor. What a mess.

Speaking of surprising noises, the Israelite people used loud sounds to bring down the city of Jericho in today's Bible story. They had finally reached the Promised Land, but when they entered the land, they encountered Jericho. Jericho had really tall walls, and when the gates were shut, there was no way into the city. It was a fortress.

Okay, so here's the scoop on Jericho. The people there didn't follow God. In fact, they actually were awful to other people. And God had given the people in Jericho many chances to follow him, but they kept refusing. So God told the people of Israel to go defeat Jericho. But they weren't going to conquer this fortress-like city in an ordinary way. Read about what happened in Joshua 6.

What kind of sound do you think the Israelites' horns made? What about the sound when Jericho's walls fell down? I can't imagine how loud it was! I wonder if the sound made the people jump like the sea salt crystals.

What's amazing about this story is that everyone in the Promised Land heard about what happened. Someone told someone else who told someone else who told someone else. They told each other about the God who had broken the walls of Jericho, a place people thought could never be defeated.

God has also called us to use our voices to tell others about him. In fact, Psalm 78:4 says this: "We will tell the next generation about the glorious deeds of the LORD, about his power and his mighty wonders." We can use the sound of our voices to tell other people about all the amazing things God has done, including the most amazing thing of all: that God sent his Son so that anyone who trusts in him will not perish but have eternal life (see John 3:16)!

Now that's something to shout about!

Collecting Your Family's Data

What happened to the salt crystals when you shouted? What about when you whispered?

Describe how different people's voices affect the crystals differently.

Do you think you would have listened if God had told you that you could defeat Jericho by walking around it and then shouting? Why or why not?

What has God done in your life that may have seemed impossible?

Prayer Time

As a family, ask God how you can use sound to tell others about Jesus. Maybe you can tell a story or sing a song or clap out a rhythm about God's love. Ask God to bring people into your life who need to hear about the mighty deeds of God.

SPAGHETTI STRENGTH

Samson
(Judges 16)

Introduction

What do you picture when you think of building materials? Steel, wood, bricks . . . spaghetti? Now, you're probably never going to ride in an elevator to the hundredth floor of a spaghetti skyscraper, but we can learn a lot of engineering concepts from "beams" of spaghetti. And today we're going to test them out by building our very own spaghetti-beam bridge!

Fizzlebop Supply List

- Box of spaghetti
- 2 objects of equal height (a pair of chairs or large cardboard boxes)
- Hole punch
- Large plastic or paper cup
- 6-in (15 cm) length of string
- Paper clip
- 100 pennies
- 2 rubber bands

The Experiment

1. Set the 2 chairs or cardboard boxes side by side. Leave a gap only 2 inches (5 cm) less than the length of a piece of spaghetti.

2. Using the hole punch, create 2 small holes right under the rim of your plastic or paper cup. The holes should be directly opposite from one another.

3. Tie the string to the holes in your cup to create a handle so the cup is like a bucket.

4. Bend the paper clip into either an S- or C-shaped hook. This hook will hang the string handle on the spaghetti bridge.

5. Set a single piece of spaghetti across the gap between your bridge supports. Hang the cup on the strand of spaghetti.

6. Record a guess in the chart below of how many pennies you think the bridge will hold.

7   Carefully add 1 penny into the cup at a time.

FIZZ TIP: Support the cup with your hand when you place a penny in it, then slowly lower the cup until the string pulls on the spaghetti.

8   Add pennies until the strand of spaghetti breaks. Record the number of pennies in your bucket at breaking point.

9   Next, bundle together 5 pieces of spaghetti by wrapping their ends with rubber bands. Repeat the weight test.

10   Try the test again with bundles of 10, 20, and 50 strands of spaghetti. (You may need to get more pennies or a larger cup!)

"Dr. Fizzlebop, what's happening?"

Did you notice where the spaghetti in each bridge broke first? Were they the strands at the bottom of the spaghetti bridge? The strands along the underside of the bridge are under the most tension (which means they are being pulled apart). The opposite of tension is **compression** (which means being pressed together). Dry spaghetti is **brittle**—it typically breaks instead of bending. And once one strand of spaghetti breaks, the others are likely to follow rapidly.

Devotional

One strand of spaghetti can hold more weight than we might think! I have to admit, when we first attempted this spaghetti experiment at Fizzlebop Labs, we were very impressed with the strength of the spaghetti. We even made our own extra-long spaghetti noodles with a pasta machine and then built a bridge for me to walk across. Sadly, we never got enough strands together to hold my weight. The bridge broke every time.

No matter how much weight one strand of spaghetti can hold, multiple strands are stronger when they're combined.

You know, that reminds me of a story from the book of Judges in the Bible. Once the people of Israel made it to the Promised Land, things didn't go so well. The people disobeyed God a lot and started worshiping all kinds of idols.

It was definitely a messy situation. And it got even worse!

Other groups of people attacked the Israelites, stole from them, and even made them slaves. When the people cried out to God for help, God sent judges—but not like judges today, who bang the gavel in a courtroom. The judges in Bible times rescued the people from their enemies—kind of like heroes.

One of those judges was a guy named Samson. Now, Samson was strong. One time, he was trapped by some enemies inside a city, and he simply tore the city gates out of the wall. God gave Samson his strength and helped Samson to rescue the people.

But Samson didn't always trust God. Often he relied on himself and his own strength instead. Eventually, some enemies of Israel called the Philistines trapped him. They led Samson in chains to a huge building where the leaders of the Philistines mocked and laughed at him.

This time, Samson turned to God for strength instead of relying on himself. And God answered Samson's prayer. He was able to push over two pillars which held up the building. The temple crashed down, and the Philistines were defeated.

Sometimes we try to do everything in our own strength, kind of like one piece of spaghetti trying to hold up tons of pennies. But when we trust in God and lean on his strength, we're more like 50 pieces of spaghetti bundled together. With God's help, we can love others, love God, and do what's right.

Collecting Your Family's Data

Number of spaghetti strands in the bridge	Guess of how many pennies the bridge can hold	Number of pennies it took to break the bridge
1		

Number of spaghetti strands in the bridge	Guess of how many pennies the bridge can hold	Number of pennies it took to break the bridge
5		
10		
20		
50		

Did you see or hear any strands of spaghetti breaking before the entire bundle of spaghetti broke?

....

Do you think the breaks are the result of compression or tension?

....

What would you do if you had strength like Samson?

....

What do you need God's help with today?

....

Prayer Time

Amazing Creator, help us to remember to do things in your strength, not ours. Help us to call on you and trust you instead of trusting in ourselves. We know you are good and strong! Amen.

FLOATING PAPER CLIP

Ruth's Commitment
(Ruth 1:16-17)

Introduction

Magnetism is a strange phenomenon. An invisible force moves another object through attraction—it almost seems like magic. Indeed, magicians use magnets in some of their tricks to move them without touch. Today we're going to observe the amazing power of magnetics with a simple paper clip and a magnet.

WARNING! This experiment requires scissors. Safety first!

Fizzlebop Supply List

- 6.5 in (16.25 cm) of string (You may trim the string later.)
- Metal paper clip
- Tape
- 32-oz (960 mL) jar with a metal lid
- Magnet (Find your strongest one.)
- Scissors

The Experiment

1. Tie the paper clip to one end of the string.

2. Tape the other end of the string to the bottom of the inside of the jar. Drop the paper clip into the jar.

3. Tape the magnet to the inside of the lid.

4. Put the lid on the jar and turn the jar upside down so that the paper clip hangs from the string.

   FIZZ TIP: If the paper clip touches the magnet, you'll need to trim a bit of string off.

5. Slowly and carefully turn the jar right-side up. Observe the paper clip as you do.

"Dr. Fizzlebop, what's happening?"

The metal paper clip you are using is likely made of steel, which is a ferrous metal. (**Ferrous** simply means the metal contains iron.) Magnets attract ferrous metals. Why? A magnetic field stimulates a ferrous metal's electrons to align, forming north and south poles. When your paper clip came within range of your magnet's magnetic field, the paper clip became attracted to the magnet. But because you tied a string to the paper clip, it couldn't reach all the way to the magnet. The force of attraction between the magnet and paper clip was stronger than gravity's pull on the paper clip, thereby keeping it suspended in the air.

Devotional

Have you heard the story of Ruth? She was not one of God's chosen people (a descendant of Abraham, Isaac, and Jacob). She was a Moabite (from a foreign country) whose Jewish husband died and left her as a young widow. Then her mother-in-law, Naomi, decided to leave Moab and return to Israel. Naomi encouraged her widowed daughters-in-law to stay in Moab with their families. One did, but Ruth chose to go with Naomi instead.

Ruth's words to Naomi, found in Ruth 1:16-17, have become famous because they demonstrate Ruth's extreme loyalty. Turn there in your Bible and read those verses for yourself.

Why would Ruth make such a serious commitment? The simple answer is magnetism. In the same way that the paper clip was drawn to the magnet, Ruth was powerfully drawn to someone. The question is, who was Ruth so powerfully drawn to? Was it her mother-in-law, Naomi? Or was it God?

Even though Naomi was bitter and sad after the deaths of her husband and sons, Ruth committed to help care for her. Together, they returned to Israel, and Ruth began picking up grain to feed Naomi and herself. A man named Boaz, who owned the field Ruth worked in, noticed how hardworking she was. Boaz did everything he could to help her, and eventually they got married and had a son named Obed. Obed later became the father of Jesse, and Jesse's youngest son was David, whom God chose as the second king of Israel. That means that Ruth became the great-grandma of King David and one of the great-great-great-greatest grandmas of Jesus!

Why did Ruth get chosen by God to be part of Jesus' family? I think it's because Ruth came to love God, who magnetically drew Ruth to himself. Then Ruth's humility, hard work, and care of Naomi attracted Boaz to her. And Boaz's kindness and generosity toward Ruth drew Ruth to Boaz. Wow—that's a whole lot of magnetism!

So, you see, as Ruth put her trust in the God of Israel, God rewarded her trust. He provided a husband and family for her and even included her in the family tree of Christ. How fizztastic is that?

Collecting Your Family's Data

How many tries did it take for the paper clip to float?

What other items could you attach to the string that might be magnetic?

If you had the world's largest magnet, what would you try to pick up?

Have you ever chosen to trust God, as Ruth did, and seen him reward your trust?

What do you need to trust God with today?

Prayer Time:

Amazing Creator, when life is hard, please help us to not grow bitter, as Naomi did. Please help us to pour out our hearts to you, especially when we feel confused and hurt. Please help us to trust you through the hard times, as Ruth did. Then let us rejoice when you provide for all our needs! Amen.

SPINNING BUCKET

David and Goliath
(1 Samuel 17)

Introduction

How's the weather outside today? Sunny? Good, 'cause you're going to want to find an open space outdoors for this water experiment. What do you think will happen if a bucket of water is turned upside down over your head? You'll get soaked, right? Well, what if you add some speed and circular motion? We're going to find out what happens while learning a thing or two about **centripetal force**. It's a stupendous force—in fact, a boy once used it to defeat a giant. So while we learn the neato science behind centripetal force, we're also going to go deeper with one of my favorite Bible stories of all time, David and Goliath.

Fizzlebop Supply List

- Small bucket with a strong handle
- Water
- An open area outside where spilling some water is okay

The Experiment

1 Fill the bucket with water until it is half full.

2 Stand clear of other people or objects and be prepared to get a little wet.

3 Hold the bucket by its handle and extend your arm.

4 Swing the bucket in a circular motion by your side (toward the sky and back toward the ground). The key is speed—if your bucket is not going fast enough, water will slop out of it.

FIZZ TIP: Ask a family member to observe what is happening with the water while you're spinning the bucket. Then switch roles!

"Dr. Fizzlebop, what's happening?"

A bucket half-full of water is spinning through the air, yet the water remains in the bucket. This is the result of centripetal force, which acts on objects moving in a circle around a center (your hand holding the bucket). Has someone ever held your hands and spun you around? Your feet pull out and away from your body (inertia trying to keep your body moving in a straight line), yet your arms are held in place by the person who is spinning you (centripetal force). Your whole body feels the pull of centripetal force directed toward the person in the center.

Devotional

Time to open your Bible! Turn to 1 Samuel 17 and read the marvelous story of David and Goliath.

Ponder this for a second: What amount of faith would you need to step in front of a giant, armed only with a stone and sling? David knew God was fighting for him, so he wasn't afraid of Goliath.

As Goliath prepared to charge David with sword, spear, and javelin, David began to swing his sling. And when his sling was swinging at super speed, he released the stone with not only magnificent force but stupendous accuracy. Down came Goliath, defeated not just by a stone and a boy—but by the God of Israel. WOW!

At first, was it hard to believe that a bucket of water could pass over your head without getting you wet? But with a little faith you tried it and hopefully succeeded. While our experiment took only a little faith, I imagine David's faith that God would see him through to victory was tremendous.

Ponder once again: Have you ever had a Goliath-sized obstacle or trial in your life, where you turned to God and asked him to see you through? If not, that's okay, but if that time ever comes, remember that you have the Champion of all champions on your side, ready to intercede for you if you trust in him. He will see you through your greatest challenges.

FIZZ FACT: The best method of launching a stone from a sling is with an underhand motion. As someone well practiced with the sling, David would have known that. This is also the method you used when you swung the bucket of water.

Collecting Your Family's Data

Describe what happened to the water in the bucket as it spun.

....

Did water spill from your bucket if you slowed it down?

....

Share a Goliath-sized challenge you have faced. What did you do to overcome it? Or are you still facing it?

....

Prayer Time

Amazing Creator, we're so grateful for your mighty hand and that you stand as our Champion even when we face trials that seem insurmountable. We pray for our courage and faith to grow, that we might be as David was when he faced Goliath. Amen.

My friends Brock Eastman and Marianne Hering wrote a book called *Showdown with the Shepherd*. It's book five in the Imagination Station series, and it's all about David and Goliath—with a little twist.

CONDENSATION

Elijah Prays for Rain

(1 Kings 18)

Introduction

Rain—it's my absolute favorite type of weather. I love the sound of it on the roof and the look of it as it falls across the sky. Rain makes many things grow—from plants to rivers—and I always enjoy walking through a lush green forest or standing by a raging waterfall. And there is nothing like the feel of a cool drizzle on your face during a morning walk. It can really clear the senses and get the mind thinking. So I thought we'd do a little experiment to see how rain forms.

WARNING! This activity requires hot water. Safety first!

Fizzlebop Supply List

- 2 cups (480 mL) hot water (close to boiling temperature)
- 32-oz (960 mL) mason jar
- Ceramic plate
- Timer (watch or phone)
- 4 ice cubes

The Experiment

1 Pour the hot water into the jar.

2 Cover the jar with the ceramic plate (faceup).

3 Set the timer for 3 minutes and wait.

4 Place the ice cubes on the plate.

5 Observe the water cycle in action.

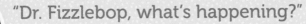

"Dr. Fizzlebop, what's happening?"

Have you ever noticed how boiling water creates steam? In today's experiment, when that steam (water as a gas) hits the cold plate above, it condenses back into water droplets. This is the same thing that happens in our atmosphere. On extremely hot, humid days, for instance, a thunderstorm often comes in the afternoon or evening. That's because as the temperature drops (especially in the colder, higher part of the atmosphere), the humid air condenses into precipitation and rains to the ground. Awfully nifty, I'd say.

Devotional

Have you ever been thirsty before? Being thirsty is such a dreadful feeling! Your mouth goes dry, your throat gets scratchy, and soon the only thing you can think about is finding a nice, refreshing cup of water. When clouds cover the sky and rain pours, you might be sad that you can't play outside with friends or enjoy the sunshine, but rain is super important to the world around us. Without rain, we wouldn't have fresh water to drink or food to eat.

But sometimes regions go through what's called a drought. A drought is a really tough time because it means that rain is not falling from the sky to provide water and keep plants alive.

During the life of the prophet Elijah, there was a three-and-a-half-year drought. You see, the people had not been following God. Instead, they had gone back to their old habits of worshiping idols. Yikes! That's not so swell!

In the book of 1 Kings (chapter 18), God tells Elijah to meet with King Ahab on top of a mountain called Mount Carmel (no, not *caramel*, like the ice-cream topping.) There, they would have a showdown to see who the real God was. The challenge was this: whichever God sent fire from heaven was the real God. Well, King Ahab's priests called on a false god named Baal for hours, asking Baal to send fire. Here's the problem though: Baal wasn't real!

Finally, it was Elijah's turn. He called on God. God sent fire immediately, and the people knew that he was the real God. Then Elijah began to pray. A few moments later, a cloud formed out over the sea. Before anyone could blink twice, rain began to fall from the sky. The drought was over!

In our experiment today, we saw water drip from the plate in a magnificent way. Did you know that God is the one who put the water cycle in place? The water cycle keeps our whole planet moving and alive. Water evaporates, becomes a gas, and forms a cloud, which then rains. The rain falls into oceans, seas, and lakes, or into rivers and streams, where it rolls back to the oceans, seas, and lakes. From there, it evaporates again. Stupendous!

God is the true, all-powerful God. God is so fizztastically smart that he came up with this whole idea of the water cycle so we would have water to drink.

Today, thank God for being real and for creating something as amazing as the scientific process called the water cycle.

Collecting Your Family's Data

When did the condensation start to form? Was it before the timer went off?

....

Describe what you saw happening in the jar.

....

Share a time when God answered one of your prayers. Are you praying for God to do anything amazing in your life right now?

....

Prayer Time

Amazing Creator, thank you for being real. You are really there, and you came up with so many amazing systems to keep our world spinning and alive! Amen.

DUSTING for FINGERPRINTS

Esther's Courage
(Book of Esther)

Introduction

Today, we're going to solve a mystery by using a marvelous technique. When I was younger, I may have dabbled in the world of amateur sleuths (which is another word for detectives). I set up my own detective agency, right out back in my clubhouse. I'd take a case on for a soda or a couple of quarters (which is how much soda cost when I was a kid). How soda got so expensive is a mystery itself. But that's not what we're learning about today. You see, people leave clues everywhere, and God made each of us unique, one of a kind, as evidenced by our fingerprints. Those unique fingerprints—and the fact that my friends often had sticky fingers—usually provided the evidence I needed to solve quite a number of mysteries in my town.

Fizzlebop Supply List

- 1 tbsp (15 mL) honey
- Drinking glass
- 5 tbsp (25 g) cocoa powder
- New soft-bristle toothbrush
- Scotch tape
- Tan, white, or yellow construction paper
- Family members (as many as are willing!)

The Experiment

1 Dab the fingers and thumb on one hand on the surface of the honey.

FIZZ TIP: Clean off any excess honey.

2 Grab hold of the drinking glass with your sticky-fingered hand. Then you can wash off the honey from your fingers.

FIZZ TIP: Make sure each of your fingers and thumb press against the glass.

3 Sprinkle cocoa powder onto the honey prints on the outside of the glass. Use the toothbrush to carefully brush away excess cocoa powder.

Tear off one piece of tape per print and place them over the dusted fingerprints.

Gently lift the pieces of tape from the glass and stick them on the construction paper. Write your name above your fingerprints.

Do this experiment with other family members. Examine each person's prints and compare your prints with theirs.

"Dr. Fizzlebop, what's happening?"

You added a bit of honey to make sure your fingerprints showed up on the glass, but even without the honey, your skin oils leave behind residue when you touch an object or surface. The powder makes visible the unique patterns of the ridges on your fingertips.

FIZZ FACT: Did you know that no two people have the same fingerprint patterns? See Isaiah 64:8 and Psalm 139:13-14 for more about how God made us each one of a kind.

Devotional

You are a stupendous creation of an amazing Creator! Did you know that? In fact, there is no one else on earth who is exactly like you. You are a completely unique human being whom God loves so much!

In today's experiment, we discovered something amazing about the way God created us: those teeny-tiny ridges on your fingers that form your fingerprints are yours alone. They're part of your identity!

Remember how I told you that I used to want to be a detective? Well, one time my friends and I wanted to solve a mystery. Somehow the vegetables from my dad's vegetable garden kept going missing! So we put on disguises to hide our identities—my disguise was some big glasses and a fake mustache—and then hid behind the old tree by my dad's garden. We watched and watched, and then we saw it. A sneaky rabbit hopped into the garden and snatched a vegetable right in front of us!

We had solved the mystery and knew we were safe to reveal our identity to the wily rabbit.

But have you heard about a woman in the Bible who didn't feel safe to tell anyone who she really was? Her name was Esther. Esther was a Jew who lived near a place called the fortress of Susa, where the king lived. She was chosen to marry the king and become the next queen. But her cousin Mordecai told her not to let anyone know that she was a Jew.

In fact, a man who worked for the king wanted to kill anyone who was a Jew. That meant Esther was in danger! Esther decided to risk it and tell the king who she really was, because she knew it was the only way she could save her people. When the king found out, he was able to help Esther and the rest of the Jews in the kingdom.

In today's world, some people who follow Jesus are nervous to tell other people they are Christians. They might be afraid someone will make fun of them—or, in some parts of the world, they could be in danger like Esther was.

But God created you for a purpose, and when you decide to follow Jesus, he "re-creates" you! In 2 Corinthians 5:17, Paul tells us, "Anyone who belongs to Christ has become a new person. The old life is gone; a new life has begun!"

When you follow God, you have a new identity: you are a Christian, and God has given you eternal life! Even when you get nervous or scared, you can stand strong as someone who is part of the family of God.

If you're a Christian, don't be afraid to tell others about your identity in Jesus. In fact, invite them to join you to be part of God's family forever!

Collecting Your Family's Data

What differences do you notice between the sets of prints?

....

How do you think dusting for fingerprints is useful for detectives solving mysteries?

....

Have you ever been nervous to tell someone you were a Christian? Why or why not?

....

Prayer Time

Amazing Creator, you've made each person in our family unique. We have some similarities, yet our differences are the result of your wonderful creativity. Help us to use our uniqueness for your purposes. Amen.

FIZZ EXTRA: Who Done It?

Keep hold of your evidence sheets (those pieces of construction paper with the fingerprints on them) for this fun FIZZ EXTRA. You've seen how unique each person's fingerprints are. Now put your powers of observation to the test with a Who Done It? challenge and uncover who left their prints at the scene of the crime.

Find the WHO DONE IT? project at Fizzlebop.com, or scan this QR Code and click or tap FIZZ EXTRA.

TORNADO in a BOTTLE

Peace amid the Whirlwind

(Job 1–2)

Introduction

I'll be the first to admit tornadoes can be scary to experience. Where I grew up, there wasn't a summer that didn't go by without the tornado siren going off at least a few times. I can remember watching an F4 tornado pass just north of my hometown. Though a large manufacturing plant was totally destroyed, all four hundred employees were safe inside a shelter. Tornadoes are powerful, destructive weather events, and in this next experiment we'll have a chance to see what one looks like. But should you ever experience one in real life, be sure to seek shelter. As always, safety first!

Fizzlebop Supply List

- 2 L (68 oz) clear bottle with a cap
- 3 tbsp (45 g) glitter
- Funnel
- 1.5 L (6 cups) water

The Experiment

1. Pour the glitter into the bottle (using the funnel).

2. Add water to the bottle (using the funnel) until it's three-fourths full.

3. Put the cap on tightly, turn the bottle upside down, and hold it by the neck.

4. Quickly spin the bottle in a circular motion for 10 seconds.

5. Observe what's happening inside. (It may take a few attempts to get it going.)

"Dr. Fizzlebop, what's happening?"

When you spin the bottle, inertia causes the swirling water to want to go in a straight line, out of the bottle.

Centripetal force pushes the water away from the walls of the bottle, toward the center. This combination causes a water **vortex** (funnel) that looks similar to a tornado. The faster the water spins, the greater the centripetal force, and the smaller the vortex. The glitter makes it easier to see the quickly spinning water.

Devotional

How would you feel if God described you like this: the finest person in all the earth, blameless—a person of complete integrity, who fears God and stays away from evil?

That'd be a magnificent feeling, right?

In the book of Job, we read about a man whom God indeed described this way. But Satan told God that Job was righteous only because he had everything he could ever want—so if God allowed Satan to take it all away, God would see that Job only worshiped him because he had a good life.

Within short order (which means quickly), Job's world was wrecked. First his livestock and servants were all stolen or destroyed, and then came the great wind—perhaps a tornado—that destroyed the home of Job's oldest son, killing all of Job's children. The devastation was overwhelming.

What do you think Job did? Do you think he got angry and blamed God? Read Job 1:20-22 to find out.

In spite of all the disasters he had just faced, Job still worshiped God. He was not prideful, and he knew that everything in his life really belonged to God. He also realized that all the wondrous things he possessed were nothing compared to what he would have in heaven.

We can find more insight into Job's view of his earthly wealth in the New Testament. Turn to Matthew 6:19-21. What do these verses say about the best place to keep our treasure?

Ponder ways you could share your blessings with others who may not have as much. Why not turn your eyes and thoughts to heaven and begin storing your treasures there instead of keeping them all in your piggy bank? Look for ways to give abundantly to those around you in need, and you'll soon find a treasure that no tornado can sweep away.

Collecting Your Family's Data

What did you observe about the shape of the water vortex?

....

Why do you think the vortex was wider at the top and narrower at the bottom?

....

What does it mean to store your treasures in heaven?

....

How can you and your family begin storing treasures in heaven instead of on earth?

....

Prayer Time

Amazing Creator, help our family to turn our eyes to heaven. Help us to be grateful for what we have but to rely on you, not on our material possessions. Show us ways to abundantly bless those in need with what you've abundantly entrusted to us. Amen.

Storing Treasures in Heaven

Put Matthew 6:19-21 into action by spending time as a family serving your community. You're in for a fizztastic time of family fun and that fizzilicious feeling you can only get when you give selflessly.

Take on this **FIZZ EXTRA** and share God's abundant blessings with your neighbors.

Find the **STORING TREASURES IN HEAVEN** project at Fizzlebop .com, or scan this QR code and click or tap **FIZZ EXTRA**.

RIVERBED EROSION

Rock and Refuge

(Psalm 31:2)

Introduction

Have you ever seen the Mississippi River? It's this marvelously long and at times wondrously wide river that flows north to south near the middle of the United States. It has a nickname—"the Mighty Mississippi"—which is accurate, but you could also call it the "Mighty *Muddy* Mississippi." Say that three times fast! A vast amount of water flows down the Mississippi River. It's muddy because as all that water runs its course, it pulls dirt, rocks, and trees from along its banks. Water is powerful, and it has the power to move or erode almost anything in its path. And that's where our experiment comes in!

Fizzlebop Supply List

- **2 hardback books**
- **Baking sheet with sides**
- **1/2 lb (200 g) sand**
- **Pencil**
- **1/2 lb (200 g) small rocks (pebbles)**
- **2 rocks about the size of an egg**
- **6 sticks about 2 in (5 cm) in height**
- **2 cups (480 mL) water**

The Experiment

1. Stack the books on a hard surface. Then set one end of the baking sheet on the books, creating a gentle slope.

2. Pour the sand all over the baking sheet.

3. Lightly drag the pencil through the sand, making the shape of an S. This is your riverbed.

4. Place pebbles along the riverbed.

5. Position the 2 larger rocks on the baking sheet so they overlap with the riverbed.

6. Lay 3 sticks (representing trees) across the riverbed and place the rest of the sticks near the edge of the riverbed.

7 Slowly pour water into the highest point of the riverbed. Observe what happens.

8 Now pour the water more quickly. Observe.

"Dr. Fizzlebop, what's happening?"

As rain falls, rivers flow. And as water flows along a riverbed, it slowly erodes the banks of the river. Soil, rocks, trees, and anything along the path can get pulled into the river and pushed or floated downstream due to **erosion**. As you add water to your riverbed, bits of sand, pebbles, and "trees" will begin to move. Over time—and with enough water—even the boulders would end up moving downstream.

Devotional

Have you ever been enjoying the beach when all of a sudden a big wave knocked you off your feet? If you're like me, you might panic inside until you get your feet under you. Uggghhh! I do *not* like the icky taste of salt water. Blehhh!

Sometimes life feels calm and peaceful, and you're as happy as a kid making mud pies by a stream. Then suddenly a flash flood of wild events sweeps through the riverbed of your life and erodes your peace. Know what I'm talking about?

Life happens. Sometimes it's really tough. In times like that, we might wish we could escape the turmoil and return to solid ground.

That's why I love Psalm 31:2, in which David cries out to God with these words:

Turn your ear to listen to me;
    rescue me quickly.
Be my rock of protection,
    a fortress where I will be safe.

Can you picture a lighthouse, sitting on a rocky island a ways off the coast? Waves crash against the rocks repeatedly, but the rocks stand firm and keep the lighthouse from being washed away. The architect of that lighthouse chose that rocky island for a reason. It's solid and strong, and it can't be eroded like the sandy beach.

That lighthouse is a beacon to sailors on boats out at sea, whether to warn them of shallow reefs or guide them to a bay during a terrible storm. But that lighthouse can only stand and do its job because it is firmly on the solid rock. The same is true for us. When we have a firm foundation in God (our rock), then we can shine brightly for him. We can guide others safely into his arms or even warn them of dangers in their paths.

Collecting Your Family's Data

What changed once you started pouring more water into the riverbed?

....

Which objects (sand, pebbles, sticks, rocks) moved the most? Why do you think that happened?

....

What problems are eroding your life or peace right now?

....

How can you be sure that you won't be swept away by life's floods?

....

Prayer Time

Amazing Creator, thank you that you always hear us when we call. You love to keep us safe when challenges crash over us like waves! We can run to you at any time, and you will be our reliable solid ground. Amen.

COFFEE FILTER PARACHUTES

God's Protection
(Psalm 91:1)

Introduction

I'm ecstatic about today's experiment. Coffee is one of my favorite drinks, second only to sparkling water—because, after all, what is in sparkling water? Fizz, of course! We won't be drinking any coffee for our experiment, but we *will* be using a coffee filter to create a parachute. The science behind parachutes is awfully nifty!

Fizzlebop Supply List

- Coffee filter
- Ruler
- Pencil
- Watercolor paint (6 colors)
- Paintbrush
- Hole punch
- Scissors
- String
- Paper clip
- 3 pipe cleaners
- Tape measure
- Timer (watch or phone)

The Experiment

1. Lay the coffee filter flat and use the ruler and pencil to divide it into 6 equal portions.

2. Paint each section a separate color and let it dry.

3. Punch 6 holes along the outer edge of the coffee filter where the colored sections meet.

4. Cut 6 10-inch (25 cm) pieces of string. Tie the end of a string through each of the holes. (One string per hole.) Then tie the loose ends of the six strings together.

5. Hook the paper clip above the knot and secure it.

6. Make a person out of the pipe cleaners. Use one for the head and body, one for the arms, and one for the legs.

7. Take the end of the paper clip not attached to the knot and attach it just under the arms of your pipe-cleaner person.

8. Find somewhere to drop the parachute and measure the height from which you are going to release it. Time how long it takes for the parachute to touch down.

9. Release the parachute several times from the same height and record how long it takes to touch down each time.

"Dr. Fizzlebop, what's happening?"

When you released the parachute, the pipe-cleaner person acted as a weight and pulled down on the strings. This helped open up the large surface area of the coffee filter, creating **air resistance**, which slowed down the descent of the parachute. Try this experiment again using different types of materials for the parachute, a larger surface area, and different **payloads** (what the parachute is carrying), such as a pen with a clip on it, an empty soda can, or an action figure. Observe what happens when you make these changes.

Devotional

It's important for pilots to have a parachute just in case they need to make a safe escape from a plane that can no longer fly. In the same way, you might one day need God's help during a challenging situation. And guess what? God will always be there for you. Isn't that fizztastic?

Let's get out our magnifying glasses and take a closer look at Psalm 91:1, which my dad read to me when I was a scared ten-year-old.

How can we "live in the shelter of the Most High"? Do we need GPS to get there? Actually, the great news is that God's shelter is very close. Any time you're lonely or hurt or scared, God knows it. The Father knows exactly what you're feeling, and the Spirit of God is praying for you. God stands ready to offer you the parachute of his invisible, comforting presence.

How do I know? Because I've spent a lot of time in the shelter of the Most High, which is both a real place and a place that I like to imagine as best I can. You can imagine it too.

In your mind, what does that shelter look like? A parachute when you're falling? A mighty stone fortress? A cozy living room? I like to picture myself curled up in Father God's lap, safe and secure and gently held.

And you know what's the most splendid thing about it? When I picture myself in the Father's lap, I don't need to say a single word. I don't have to explain myself, 'cause he already knows. He's zealous in his love for me, so he wants to be closer than anyone else.

Have you ever felt like you or your problems were too much for someone? It's never like that with God. He wants us to come to him with every joy, every pain, every hope, and every ache. We can always find rest in the shadow of the Almighty, knowing God will keep us safe in the midst of scary circumstances. Isn't that wondrous?!

Collecting Your Family's Data

Height	Time to Ground

Did your parachute take the same time to touch down on every drop? If not, what factors might have changed?

....

Did your parachute fall straight down or did it float away?

....

What are you dealing with that you're glad God already knows about?

....

What would you like God to shelter and protect you from? Have you "snuggled into" his shadow?

....

Prayer Time

Amazing Creator, thank you for taking care of us and keeping us safe. Please help us remember that you already know everything we're dealing with, and you care! We might need to talk to you about it sometimes, or we might just want to rest, knowing you've got this. Thank you! Amen.

LAVA LAMP

God's Word Is a Lamp
(Psalm 119:105)

Introduction

Greetings! Today's experiment is fabulously fizztastic: we're going to build a lava lamp! Now, don't worry—it doesn't use real lava from a volcano. Our experiment will *look* like lava, though, and it'll even teach us about density. And the best thing is, we're going to use a little bit of my favorite thing to help—fizz.

WARNING! This experiment requires a knife. Safety first.

Fizzlebop Supply List

- Clean 20-oz (600 mL) plastic bottle (label removed) with cap
- Funnel
- 1 3/4 cups plus 3 tbsp (450 mL) water
- 1/2 cup plus 2 tbsp (150 mL) vegetable oil
- Food coloring
- Seltzer tablets
- Knife

FIZZ TIP: You can make your lava lamp out of any size bottle—just fill the bottle ¾ full of water and ¼ full of oil.

93

The Experiment

1 Remove the lid to the bottle and insert the funnel into the opening. Pour the water down the funnel.

2 Pour the oil down the funnel. Remove the funnel and watch as the oil and water separate.

3 Add 12 drops of food coloring to the mixture. Choose any color you like.

FIZZ TIP: If your oil is yellow, you may want to avoid yellow or orange food coloring, as these colors will be challenging to see.

4 Cut the seltzer tablets into 4 to 6 smaller pieces.

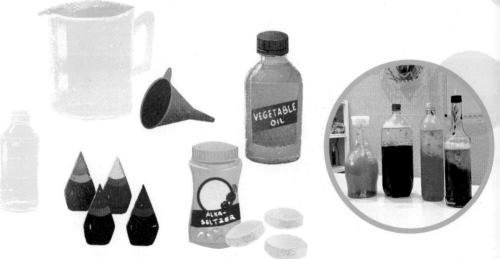

5. Drop 1 piece into the bottle and watch as things get *fizzy* inside! Repeat this with the remaining tablets.

6. Lastly, if you can fit an entire seltzer tablet through the opening of the bottle, drop one in and enjoy the fizztastic motion.

FIZZ TIP: This lava lamp can be reused over and over. Simply seal the bottle and store. When you're ready for more fizzy fun, take out the bottle and drop in another seltzer tablet. And the fizziness will start again!

"Dr. Fizzlebop, what's happening?"

The oil and water separate because oil is less dense than water. As the seltzer tablets dissolve and release **carbon dioxide** gas, the bubbles take some of the colored water to the surface with them. When the bubbles reach the surface, they burst. The colored water sinks back to the bottom of the bottle. This creates a movement of colors up and down throughout the bottle.

Devotional

Where is your Bible right now? Is it on your shelf, next to your bed, or on a device? Take a moment to find it.

Now turn to Psalm 119:105. This verse tells us that the book you hold in your hands—whether physical or digital—is a lamp. But not the same kind as the lava lamp you just made! It's there to guide you, to show the way, even in the dark.

Life is full of ups and downs. When things are going swell for me, I sometimes spend less time in the Bible, or I don't pay close attention during my devotions. I might even shorten my prayer time or let a distraction get in the way.

If I've been out of my devotional routine, I might not know the best way forward when faced with a challenge. I found a turtle once in my backyard. She had an awesome green and brown shell. I named her Mary Shelley after one of my favorite authors. Anyhow, I was excited because I'd never seen a turtle roaming freely before. I found a box, grabbed some lettuce from the fridge, and put a dish of water in the box for her.

But the next day, I saw a poster on a streetlight pole. It said "Missing Turtle" in big, bold letters. However, the picture was black-and-white, and the turtle's name was Lightning. Mary Shelley was green and brown, and she was by no means fast, so this couldn't be the same turtle. I decided I'd just keep her, and I ignored the voice in my head.

The next day, the voice didn't say to return the turtle but instead to open my Bible. It had been a few days, maybe a week, so a few more days wouldn't hurt, right? I left my Bible on the shelf.

Well, when I got downstairs, I found my mom at the kitchen table with her Bible open. I sat down, and as she went to put some blueberry pancakes on my plate, I glanced at a note she had written in her journal: James 4:17, "Remember, it is sin to know what you ought to do and then not do it."

That's when I felt like I'd been clobbered with a hundred-pound turtle shell. I was lying to myself. Mary Shelley was indeed Lightning, and I needed to return her to her rightful owner.

You see, the lamp guiding me didn't seem as bright to me because I wasn't choosing to illuminate my life with it. I'd been neglecting my daily reading. And so even though deep down I knew I should return the turtle, I chose to give into my desire to keep her. I wasn't fueling the light in my life.

The Bible is the lamp we should use to guide our path. When we live in his Word daily, we consume the promises, the knowledge, and the grace God offers. And when a problem comes our way, whether in a friendship or a failed experiment, God's bright lamp will help us see the way through that dark moment.

So that lava lamp you made today can be a reminder. Set it on a bookshelf or dresser in your room, and when you see it, remember to rely on the true lamp—the one that will light your way no matter what.

Collecting Your Family's Data

What did you notice about the water and oil when you first put them in the bottle?

....

What happened when you added the droplets of food coloring? What about when you added the first seltzer tablet?

....

What does it mean that God's Word is a lamp to guide your feet?

....

What does it look like to rely on God's Word in your life?

....

Prayer Time

Make a simple request that God will help you find time each day to read your Bible and pray. As a family, commit to keeping God's lamp vibrantly lit in your home.

DANCING WORMS

Praise Him with Song and Dance

(Psalm 149:2-4)

Introduction

Have you ever seen worms dance? Well, today we at Fizzlebop Labs are going to make it happen with a little help from my favorite wondrous ingredient: fizz. No live worms will be involved in this experiment, just a handful of gummy ones. So gather everyone together and let's have some fizztastic fun!

WARNING! This experiment requires a knife. Safety first!

Fizzlebop Supply List

- Knife
- Gummy worms
- 2 16-oz (480 mL) mason jars
- 1 1/4 cups (300 mL) water
- 3 tsp (15 g) baking soda
- Spoon
- 1 1/4 cups (300 mL) vinegar

The Experiment

1 Cut the gummy worms in half lengthwise.

2 Fill the first jar with the water.

3 Add the baking soda and stir.

4 Add worms and let them soak for at least 15 minutes.

5 Fill your second jar with the vinegar.

6 Remove the worms from the baking soda jar and drop them into the vinegar jar. Observe what happens.

7 Discard the worms afterward—don't eat them!

"Dr. Fizzlebop, what's happening?"

The gummy worms are dancing because of a chemical reaction between the baking soda and vinegar.

When these two mix, they produce carbon dioxide gas. Thousands of teeny-tiny carbon dioxide bubbles release and attach to each gummy worm. As those little bubbles slide across the surface of the worm, they connect and form larger bubbles. The bigger bubbles lift part of the gummy worm, and when the bubbles detach, the worm sinks back down to the bottom of the jar. Voilà! (which is French for "There you have it!") Dancing gummy worms!

Devotional

Have you ever been so joyful that your feet started to move, your hands rose into the air, and you couldn't stop shouting with glee (which is another word for happiness)? It's happened to me on more than one wondrous occasion, and honestly it probably happens a few fizztastic times each day. I promise it's not the fizz or the coffee—it's knowing that we've got a God who is so great and amazing that he created this whole earth and how it all works.

I think of Fizzlebop Labs as a place where faith meets science. You see, I know without a doubt that God made the world we live in. So when I do an experiment and see the results, I can't help but jump with joy knowing it's all part of a grand design, and I get to be part of it.

God gives us all sorts of reasons to praise him, to be happy and joyful, to step back in awe of what he has made. Take a moment to read Psalm 149:2-4. Then look at your family around you. Look at yourself in the mirror. You were all made by his hand. You're beautiful, precious, and a joy to him. Just thinking of the fact that God used his hands to mold me makes me ecstatic!

Sometimes I also think about King David and how enthusiastically he worshiped God. In 2 Samuel 6:14, we read, "David danced before the LORD with all his might."

"With all his might"! What a marvelous thought! The king of Israel dancing for God and not holding anything back. Wow! David knew as I do—and as you do too—that we have reason to celebrate, to praise, to worship.

Ponder the world you live in—its beauty, its **magnitude**, and the intricacies (which means details) that are woven into everything. All this came from one God, who is in heaven looking down at you, his creation, and smiling zealously.

I'm just so ecstatic right now, I have to do a little happy dance—and you should too!

Collecting Your Family's Data

How quickly did your gummy worms start to dance?

....

Did certain colors of gummy worms dance more than others? Do you think sour gummy worms would dance any differently? Give it a try!

....

List several things in the world that amaze you (animals, places, people). What about these things is so amazing?

....

List a few things God has done in your life that make you joyful and ready to dance or sing.

....

Prayer Time

Amazing Creator, wow! You created the entire universe, and you created us. You delight in us as your children and give us reason to praise and worship you every day. We ask you to give each of us a spirit of joy and help us to celebrate the beauty in the world you designed. Amen.

ROCK CANDY JEWELS

Wisdom

(Proverbs 3:13-26)

Introduction

Rocks and candy seem incongruous (which means they don't appear to fit together at all). It's like mud pies—a pie should be delicious and filled with fruit, or if you're my Great-Aunt Lois, with chocolate. But mud? Never. And so you ask, "Rock candy? Is this a trick?" Nope, because we are going to use sugar as our main ingredient, and sugar is made up of crystals. When a lot of sugar crystals are combined, they form a big, hard structure, which simulates the structure of certain rocks! At the end of this experiment, though, I promise you'll have a wondrous sweet treat that tastes nothing like the average rock.

WARNING! This experiment requires hot water. Safety first!

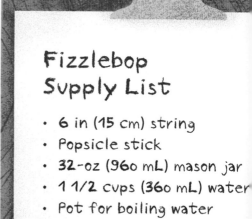

Fizzlebop Supply List

- 6 in (15 cm) string
- Popsicle stick
- 32-oz (960 mL) mason jar
- 1 1/2 cups (360 mL) water
- Pot for boiling water
- 3 cups (600 g) sugar
- Spoon
- Food coloring (optional)
- Paper towel or coffee filter

FIZZ TIP: The above supplies will create one large piece of rock candy. Gather additional supplies if you wish to create multiple sweet treats.

The Experiment

1 Tie one end of the string to the middle of the Popsicle stick.

2 Rest the Popsicle stick across the mouth of the jar and lower the string into the jar.

FIZZ TIP: The string should not touch any part of the jar. If it touches the bottom, roll the Popsicle stick to shorten the string.

3 Now that the string and Popsicle stick are ready, remove them from the jar and set them aside.

4 Pour the water into the pot and bring it to a boil.

5 Add ¼ cup (50 g) of sugar to the boiling water and stir until it dissolves. Repeat this step until all 3 cups of the sugar are dissolved. Since you are making a supersaturated solution, this process may take time. But that's part of the science.

FIZZ TIP: You can add a few drops of food coloring to the mixture to make your rock candy colorful.

6   Carefully pour the hot sugar solution into the jar, filling it nearly to the top.

7   Lower the string into the jar, with the Popsicle stick lying flat across the jar's opening. Put the jar someplace where it will not be disturbed and allow it to cool.

FIZZ TIP: Place a paper towel or coffee filter over the top of the jar so nothing falls in.

8   Now it's time to practice patience and observe. Over the next several days, your crystals will start to grow, and continue to grow.

9   When the cluster of crystals has grown nice and large, you can remove it from the jar. Cut off the string just below the Popsicle stick and give your rock candy stick a lick. Delicious, I hope!

"Dr. Fizzlebop, what's happening?"

When the water and sugar were mixed together, they formed a solution. To get it to the point of **supersaturation**, though, it was necessary to heat the water. As the water cooled, the sugar began to solidify into crystals on the string.

Devotional

While there probably isn't a treasure chest buried in your backyard, I have stupendous news for all of us! We can open and access something better than silver, gold, and jewels—any day of the week!

Just take a look at Proverbs 3:13-26 to learn more about it. As you read, ask yourself, *What is the treasure chest?* You'll want to pay close attention to words like *joyful, silver, gold, rubies, jewels, happy, safe,* and *riches.*

Did you figure it out? What is the treasure chest that holds the greatest jewels we could ever find on this earth?

If you said wisdom, you're right! And let me just be honest with you, okay? When I was a kid and heard about this treasure, I thought it sounded kinda lame. Though my parents, grandparents, aunts, uncles, cousins, neighbors, teachers, pastor, coaches, and even the mailman gave me wise advice on life, I didn't always listen. I went to church and I knew God, but I struggled to really dig into the Bible and use the wisdom within it. Sometimes it was because I thought I knew better, and sometimes I didn't like the answers I found.

I spent many an afternoon at my grandparents' house. In the kitchen, there was a drawer where my grandpa stashed his corn curls. They were cheesy, delicious, and very, very orange. Anyhow, my grandpa always shared with us at lunch even though he acted like he didn't want to. My grandma would always warn us that too much of any junk food would make us feel sick.

But I knew better. So when my grandparents were occupied and I was supposed to be playing, I snuck back into the kitchen, opened that drawer, and chowed down. The bag was empty before I knew it. I snuck back from the kitchen to the front porch where all the games were. Free and clear, and full, very full.

A short time later, my stomach started doing somersaults. It ached, and it grumbled in a bad way. I went to find my grandpa and told him I didn't feel very good.

A half smile came over his face. "Did you eat too much of something?"

Now my heart joined my stomach in feeling not so great. I knew what I'd done, but did Grandpa? Even though I'd made a bad choice earlier, I made a good choice now and confessed.

My grandpa smiled at me, "Phineas, I'm glad you told the truth." Then he took out his hankie and wiped my face. The hankie came away bright orange. *So he'd known all along.*

My grandma was wise when she'd warned me about junk food. The Bible also gives us all sorts of wondrous insight about life, but how often do we ignore it? Or maybe we haven't taken the time to read it, so we don't even know the marvelous advice inside.

Looking back, I sure wish I would have read the Bible more often. Doing so would have saved me a lot of trouble, some heartache, and at least one stomachache.

I hope you'll be smarter than I was—and wiser. If you choose the riches of wisdom now, you'll be able to avoid a lot of mistakes and live a joyful life! That doesn't mean life won't be tough at times, but you'll have the wisdom you need to handle challenges and find your way.

Collecting Your Family's Data

On what day did you first notice crystals forming? Where on the string did they begin to form?

Describe the shape and look of your crystals.

In what part of life do you need wisdom right now?

Why does the book of Proverbs say wisdom is more valuable than riches?

Prayer Time

Wow, God! It's fizztastic that we get to search for treasure in your Word and find it. We can't wait to find the jewels we need for our life and use them to get us out of sticky situations. Please help us never give up on our search for the treasure of wisdom. Other jewels may glitter and sparkle, but it seems those always turn out to be cheap fakes. We want the real treasure that only you offer. Amen.

SOAPY THUNDERHEAD

Even in Life's Storms

(Proverbs 10:25)

Introduction

Super-simple and soapy—that's the way to describe today's nifty experiment! Have you ever stood outside on a muggy (which means humid) summer day right before a storm? The sky is dark in the distance, an ominous shade of navy blue or green. Cutting across the top of the blue is a row of billowing white clouds. They're growing taller and wider. An occasional flash of neon-blue or sizzling white lightning accentuates (which means emphasizes) the clouds. A storm is coming, and the thunderhead (as those clouds are called) is growing. Sounds dramatic, but you need only three items for this experiment.

WARNING! This experiment requires high heat. Safety first!

Fizzlebop Supply List

- Bar of Ivory soap
- Large microwave-safe bowl
- Microwave

The Experiment

1. Place the bar of soap in the bowl.

2. Microwave the soap for 2 minutes on high.

3. Observe the growing thunderhead.

4. Wait 2 more minutes for the bowl and soap foam to cool.

5. Remove from the microwave and make some more observations.

6. Save the soapy thunderhead for a **FIZZ EXTRA** experiment.

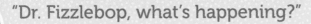

"Dr. Fizzlebop, what's happening?"

We suggested Ivory soap for this experiment because it has lots of very tiny air bubbles. When these air bubbles are heated by the microwave, they expand. Since the bar of soap is a solid, once it grows in size, it will remain that way (though some of the air bubbles will collapse and the soap thunderhead may shrink a bit). It is wondrous to see how heat and air can change the form and size of a solid.

Devotional

Picture again that storm approaching in the distance: the clouds towering higher and higher, growing like the soapy thunderhead in your microwave. Flashes of white, rumbles of thunder, the smell of rain. The storm will be here soon. What should you do? Take shelter? Comfort each other? Trust God? You should do all those things.

What about when a different kind of storm comes, one that disrupts your entire life?

When I was twelve, my mom got sick—really sick. I was scared. This big, frightening storm, but not the weather kind, swept into my world and disrupted everything. Things at home that I took for granted began to change, like eating dinner as a family, spending time with my friends, getting new gadgets or experiment materials, and even receiving the usual attention from my parents. You see, the disruption forced our family to refocus how we spent our money and even how our family spent the little time remaining after work and doctor's appointments.

I remember my mom and dad's faith—their prayers—along with the prayers of our family, our church, our friends. I witnessed how important belief and prayer were. People brought meals and groceries to our house. Family and friends watched my sister and me and made sure we got to do normal kid things. Sometimes, anonymous gifts of money would show up to help with expenses. Someone even bought us a new washer and dryer. I witnessed what Christ living in people authentically (which means truly) looked like.

My mom did get better, and our lives began to return to a new normal. But my perspective on life was forever changed, and my understanding of what it means to be Christlike had too. I saw people of faith—people who loved God—give selflessly to my family even though they owed us nothing and would not gain anything by helping us. My parents had faith that God would see us through, and he did in a way only our Amazing Creator could: *marvelously*.

Proverbs 10:25 says, "When the storms of life come, the wicked are whirled away, but the godly have a lasting foundation."

Storms don't always pass without leaving damage, and events don't always turn out the way we hope and pray for. Though my story turned out okay, even if it hadn't, I saw God working through his people. He showed my twelve-year-old self that when we ground ourselves in God and trust him, he will provide.

So I challenge you to think about people in your community who might be praying right now for God's help. How can you be his hands and feet in the storms of those around you?

Collecting Your Family's Data

What did you notice about how the soap expanded (speed, shape, size)?

What did the soap feel like (once it cooled down) compared to how it felt in bar form? What changes (if any) did you notice in smell?

Write down some ways God has provided during a storm in your life.

Prayer Time

Amazing Creator, help us to trust you even in life's storms. Help us to prepare by reading the Bible, speaking with you each day, and surrounding ourselves with other Christians who believe and trust in you. Reveal people in our lives whom we might be able to help or talk to about you. Amen.

FIZZ EXTRA: Clean Clay

So that Soapy Thunderhead looked really neato as it expanded and grew from a simple bar of soap. Now, by simply adding some toilet paper—yes, toilet paper—to the expanded bar of soap, we can conduct another super-simple experiment! Woohoo!

Create your own Clean Clay with this FIZZ EXTRA, and discover your sculpting skills.

Find the CLEAN CLAY project at Fizzlebop.com, or scan this QR code and click or tap FIZZ EXTRA.

TURNING PENNIES GREEN

Green with Envy
(Proverbs 14:30)

Introduction

Greetings, and welcome to Fizzlebop Labs! Have you ever seen the Statue of Liberty, whether in person or in a picture or video? The Statue of Liberty is magnificent to behold—she stands alone on an island, and many view her as a symbol of freedom and a welcoming beacon to people from all over the world. You may not realize it, but when you look at the statue, you're also seeing the results of a chemical reaction! (More on that in a bit.)

FIZZ FACT: Did you know there is a smaller replica of the Statue of Liberty in France? France gave the United States the Statue of Liberty in 1886, while Americans gave the city of Paris the quarter-scale replica in 1889. It's a symbol of both nations' independence and ideals of freedom. Neato!

Fizzlebop Supply List

- Paper towels
- 1/2 cup (120 mL) vinegar
- Baking sheet
- 30 pennies (a mix of old and new)
- 5 tbsp (85 g) salt

The Experiment

1 Soak several paper towels in vinegar, enough to line the bottom of the baking sheet.

FIZZ TIP: If the ½ cup (120 mL) of vinegar is not enough, you can add more.

2 Place the pennies on the paper towels.

3 Sprinkle the salt over the pennies.

4 Set the pan of pennies aside and wait. Check the pennies in 3 hours and record your observations. Then check the pennies again the next day and do the same.

FIZZ TIP: If you'd like to get your green pennies looking shiny and new again, check out the experiment on pages 242–244: "Clean Pennies with Vinegar."

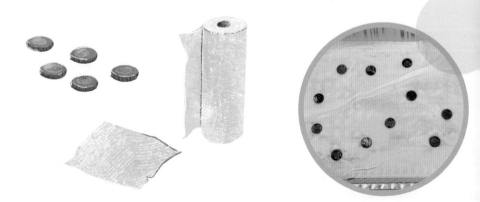

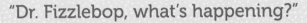

"Dr. Fizzlebop, what's happening?"

You see all that green? Well, that means a chemical reaction has occurred! Pennies contain or are plated with copper, depending on the year they were made. The vinegar (which is an **acid**) on the paper towel helps the copper in the pennies to react with the oxygen in the air, forming the blue-green color (patina) you see on each penny. This blue-green color is from a compound called malachite.

This experiment demonstrates how the Statue of Liberty changed color as well. Since it's also made of copper and exposed to the air, over time the copper and oxygen continued to react, changing the statue from a copper color to the blue-green shade you see today.

FIZZ FACT: There are many examples around the world of copper monuments that have turned green, including Berlin Cathedral Church in Germany, Statues of Heroes Square in Hungary, Belvedere Palace in Vienna, the Statues of the Apostles at Notre Dame Cathedral in France, and the statue of Sancarlone in Italy. (Look them up online!) You can even check out a statue that was built in India in 2013 and is expected to turn from copper to green over the next 100 years: Sardar Patel's Statue of Unity. It'll give you a glimpse of what the Statue of Liberty looked like when it was first built.

Devotional

Have you ever heard the phrase "green with envy"? I don't know who said it first or when it came to be. But what do you think it means to be green with envy?

Here are a few things that have made me envious in the past: a microscope, a pair of sloth socks, my friend's electric bicycle, how much prize money another scientist won for a new invention, and even how much my mom loved our cat Muffin. It's natural for us to have feelings of envy from time to time—what's important is how we handle those feelings.

Hebrews 13:5 says, "Don't love money; be satisfied with

what you have. For God has said, 'I will never fail you. I will never abandon you.'" And according to Proverbs 14:30, "A peaceful heart leads to a healthy body; jealousy is like cancer in the bones."

What should you do when you experience feelings of envy? First, pray and ask God to help you. God promises to never fail or abandon us. He gives us all we need and knows what we truly *do* need.

Look around and take note of the ways God has blessed you. When I think about it, I realize that even though I was envious of some of the fizztastic things my friends and family had, God has blessed me in other ways. Like with my telescope that I can use to see Mars, my dinosaur-eating-a-taco socks, my orange-and-blue hoverboard (which was a bit tricky to use at first), that plaque on my wall congratulating me for my extraordinary artwork on the Fizz Fountain in Wooshieville Park—and even the card from my mom telling me she is so proud of me and loves me more than the sun, moon, and stars! I guess I have been truly blessed.

All right, join with me and try this: raise your hands in the air—yep, as high as you can. Close your eyes and say, "Thank you, God, for all you do and all you will do. May you bless my family and me so we may bless others with your abundance."

Ask God to help you focus on all the ways he's shown his love to you and your family! When we remember all the good things God has done for us—instead of thinking about the things we don't have—it's easier to point other people to the Amazing Creator of all good gifts.

FIZZ FACT: For a story about how envy came between two brothers and had terrible results, read Genesis 4:3-12. This true story is an example of the consequences of allowing envy to take hold in your heart and mind.

Collecting Your Family's Data

Time Elapsed	Observations
Immediately after sprinkling the salt	
3 hours with salt	
24 hours with salt	

Describe what happened to the pennies over the course of the experiment.

....

Do you think other acids (lemon juice or orange juice) would work as well as vinegar did?

....

When was the last time you were jealous of someone or something?

....

What can you do to be content with what God has given you?

....

Prayer Time

Amazing Creator, thank you for promising never to fail or abandon us. Help us to know that what you give will always be more than we need. Amen.

ICE CREAM in a BAG

Gracious Words
(Proverbs 16:24)

Introduction

In this nifty experiment, we're going to make a delicious dessert: ice cream! What's your favorite flavor? Mine is mint chocolate chip. Today we're going to start with a couple simple flavors of ice cream, but once you see the science behind it, you can get more and more creative. There are endless possibilities! Who knows, maybe one of you is a future ice cream *glacier* (French for "ice cream maker") or *gelataio* (Italian for "ice cream maker"). Those two words sound a bit more sophisticated than the English term for someone who makes ice cream, which is simply *ice cream maker*.

Fizzlebop Supply List

- 1/2 cup (120 mL) milk
- 1/2 cup (120 mL) half-and-half
- 1/4 tsp (1 mL) vanilla extract or 2 tbsp (30 mL) chocolate syrup
- 4 tsp (20 g) sugar
- Quart-size (1 L) ziplock freezer bag
- 6 cups (1440 mL) ice cube
- Gallon-size (4 L) ziplock freezer bag
- 1/2 cup (250 g) rock salt
- Gloves (optional)

FIZZ TIP: You can find rock salt at the grocery or hardware store.

FIZZ TIP: Once you complete the experiment, you can add additional ingredients like chocolate candies, gummy worms, or bits of peppermint.

The Experiment

1. Pour milk, half-and-half, vanilla or chocolate syrup, and sugar into the quart-size (1 L) ziplock bag, and zip it shut.

   FIZZ TIP: Double check that the bag is closed all the way.

2. Measure 1 cup (240 mL) of ice and pour it into the gallon-size (4 L) ziplock bag.

3. Sprinkle a handful of rock salt over the ice.

4. Place the ingredient bag (milk, half-and-half, flavoring, sugar) into the ice-filled bag.

5. Add more ice and salt to the ice-filled bag until the bag is almost full.

6. Zip the ice-filled bag shut, and carefully hold opposite sides of the bag.

   FIZZ TIP: Double-check that this bag is closed all the way too.

7 Shake the bag back and forth for 7 to 8 minutes or until you notice the liquid becoming thick.

FIZZ TIP: You may get tired, so be ready to hand the bag off to a family member, but don't stop shaking. If your hands start getting cold, put on a pair of gloves and keep going!

8 Open the ice-filled bag and take out the ingredient bag. Rinse off the ingredient bag with cold running water to remove any salt that may be near the bag's opening.

9 Observe what's inside. Then open and do a taste test.

"Dr. Fizzlebop, what's happening?"

Get ready for a big word: **endothermic**. This term refers to a process in which an object (in this case, the ice) borrows heat from other objects (milk, half-and-half, and sugar) around it. When you added salt to the ice, it lowered the freezing point of the water, which caused the ice to immediately begin to melt. Melting is an **endothermic process**, which means heat is required to change the ice from a solid to a liquid. Where does the heat come from? It comes from the ice cream mixture. Eventually the mixture gets cold enough to start freezing and turning into ice cream!

Devotional

Back in Bible times, sweets weren't as common as they are today, and ice cream hadn't been invented yet. But there was one sweet treat that everyone loved, partly because it was not easy to find or obtain: honey!

Honey takes a lot of time and hard work for bees to make, so it's rather valuable. King Solomon likely had those prized qualities of sweetness and rarity in mind when he described another precious treat in Proverbs 16:24: "Kind words are like honey—sweet to the soul and healthy for the body."

Have you ever had someone say mean words that wounded you? Me too. Sometimes it can feel like we hear more unkind words than kind ones, and more harsh criticism than praise.

I don't know who was the first to say this, but I love it: "People will forget the things you said and the things you did, but they'll never forget how you made them feel."

You probably know what it's like for words to make you feel bad. So do I. And I hope you also know what it's like to hear kind words that make you feel great! Which ones do you speak the most?

We can't always change others' expectations of us or opinions about us, but we *can* change how we let their words affect us. We can choose which words we listen to—and whose words we believe.

Jesus died to pay for our sins. He more than made up for our imperfections. In God's eyes, Jesus is enough, and he's on our side, which means we are enough too.

Once we realize that we're super valuable and precious to God, we can become people who speak kind words to others. We can praise them not only for what they do well but for who they are! And our kind words will be like honey—or ice cream!—sweet to the soul.

Collecting Your Family's Data

Describe the ice cream inside the bag (appearance, taste, texture, temperature).

....

How do you feel when someone says kind words to you? What about when someone says something unkind?

....

Have you said any unkind words that you need to apologize for? Who in your life might need to hear some kind words from you today?

....

Prayer Time

Amazing Creator, please help us to hear and believe the good things you say about us. Please help us to see ourselves as you see us, and give us eyes to see others how you see them too. Give us kind words to lovingly speak over our family and friends. We want our words to be as refreshing as ice cream on a hot summer day! Amen.

HOOP GLIDER

Soar on Wings like Eagles
(Isaiah 40:31)

Introduction

When I was very young, I wanted to be an archaeologist—at least until I learned what a paleontologist (which is a scientist who studies dinosaurs) did! But then I got a little older, and I wanted to be an aerospace engineer so I could study and design spacecraft. Airplanes and spaceships have always fascinated me, and they still do. With public and private organizations working to send humans to the moon, Mars, and beyond, the galaxy is open for exploration in new and amazing ways—with new and amazing technology. Today we're going to design an aircraft of our own and perhaps test a few variations as well. So let's get ready to take off and experiment!

WARNING! This experiment requires scissors.
Safety first!

Fizzlebop Supply List

- 3 x 5 in (7.5 x 12.5 cm) index card
- Pencil
- Ruler
- Crayons
- Scissors
- Tape
- Plastic drinking straw

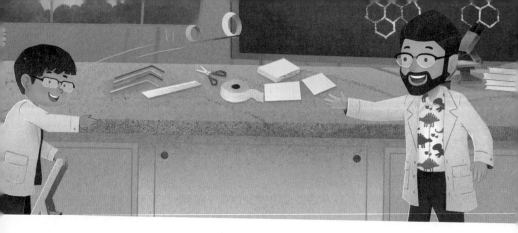

The Experiment

1. On both of the short sides of the index card, make marks at 1 inch (2.5 cm) and 2 inches (5 cm).

2. Use the ruler to trace a line between each pair of marks lengthwise, end to end.

   FIZZ TIP: Use the crayons to decorate the index card with circles or zigzags.

3. Cut along the lines to create 3 separate pieces that measure 1 inch (2.5 cm) by 5 inches (12.5 cm) each.

4. Create a hoop with 2 strips of index card: Overlap the strips by ½ inch (1.25 cm) and stick them together with a piece of tape. Next, tape together the unattached ends to complete the hoop.

5. Create a smaller hoop with the final strip of paper. Again, be sure to overlap the edges by about ½ inch (1.25 cm).

6 Lay the straw across the inside of the 2 hoops, placing the hoops at opposite ends of the straw. Tape the straw in place to attach it to the bottom of both hoops.

7 Time to launch! Hold the straw in the middle, throw the glider with the smaller hoop facing forward, and observe.
FIZZ TIP: Aim the front of the hoop glider up when throwing.

8 You can test different designs by cutting your straw shorter, making it longer by attaching 2 straws together, adding a third and fourth hoop, or simply placing the hoops at different locations on the straw.

"Dr. Fizzlebop, what's happening?"

You might have thought the hoop glider would be better at rolling than flying, but it actually has the potential to fly better than a typical paper airplane.

The different-sized hoops help balance the straw as it soars. The front hoop guides the glider. The larger hoop at the rear creates drag (which means air resistance), keeping the straw level and balanced.

Devotional

Have you ever gone bird-watching before? I really like looking for birds. I take my binoculars, a notebook, and a pencil, then search the trees near my house. So far, I've spotted about fourteen different kinds of birds that live near me! But I think one of the most magnificent birds I've ever seen was a bald eagle. Did you know that a bald eagle's wings can measure eight feet from one wing tip to the other? That's taller than me by two whole feet!

Here's another fizztastic fact from my notebook of eagle-eyed observations: eagles can fly more than 100 miles before they get tired and have to land somewhere. But I think what's even more wondrous is that eagles can dive at a speed of 100 miles per hour. Now that's stupendous!

Did you know that there's a verse in the book of Isaiah that talks about eagles? Open your Bible to Isaiah 40:31 and read it out loud.

Isaiah was a prophet who lived in the ancient land of Judah. He often delivered messages from God to the king. Some of these messages told the king what God wanted him to do, and some even told him what would happen in the future. Now, at that time Isaiah was alive, Judah was under attack a lot! In fact, Jerusalem—Isaiah's city—had to defend itself against invaders a few times.

The people living in Jerusalem were scared and wondered what to do. God gave Isaiah this message for them to remember: "Those who trust in the LORD will find new strength. They will soar high on wings like eagles. They will run and not grow weary. They will walk and not faint."

Trusting God means believing what he says and then living like it! The people needed to trust that God would be with them and help them when trouble came. When they trusted God, it was as if they could fly like eagles. It's not a coincidence that God used this powerful bird to describe those who trust in him.

God calls you to trust him too. No matter where you are, you can know that God is with you. God never leaves you or runs away from you. Whenever you need help, you can talk to God and ask. Now, God never promised to FIZZ-POOF! our problems away, but he *did* promise to lead and guide us.

Collecting Your Family's Data

Describe the path and distance of your hoop glider's flight.

....

Describe how the following changes affect the flight: length of the straw, number of hoops, and location of hoops.

....

What do you need to trust God with today?

....

Prayer Time

Take some time and think about this question: Are we trusting God? Or do we trust in other things to keep us safe and happy? Ask God this question: "God, how are we doing trusting you? Do we need to trust you more in some parts of our life?" Then ask for God's help to trust him and soar high on wings like eagles!

FIZZ EXTRA: Go the Distance

Make it a competition! Have everyone line up at the same location and throw their hoop gliders. Use a measuring tape to see whose goes the farthest.

Dr. Fizzlebop's
PREPOSTEROUS PUTTY

Potter's Clay
(Isaiah 64:8)

Introduction

Preposterous putty is a wondrous, marvelous thing. You can press it, pop it, play with it. You can roll it, rip it, and round it out. You can do almost anything with it, even copy text with it. My sister and I used to take our putty and press it against newspapers. Then, when we would pull it up, the ink from the paper would be copied onto the putty. Though on a couple of occasions my dad wasn't finished with the newspaper before we puttied it. The putty we're making today only requires two super-simple ingredients you probably already have in your house. Both ingredients are edible, so you could even eat it if you wanted to. (But I wouldn't recommend it!)

FIZZ FACT: Due to changes in printing technology and inks, newspaper printers no longer use ink that is "transferable." Try writing down some words with a pencil and transferring them with the putty you make in this experiment.

Fizzlebop Supply List

- 1 cup (240 mL) plain yogurt
- Medium mixing bowl
- 1 1/4 cups (150 g) cornstarch
- Food coloring (optional)

The Experiment

1. Put the yogurt in a medium mixing bowl.

2. Add the cornstarch to the bowl and mix the ingredients together. Keep mixing until you can roll the mixture into a ball.

3. Once a ball of putty forms, pick it up and test it to ensure the ingredients are totally combined.

   FIZZ TIP: If the putty is too dry, add a little more yogurt. If the putty is too sticky, mix in a bit more cornstarch.

4. If you'd like to make your putty colorful, add a few drops of food coloring.

"Dr. Fizzlebop, what's happening?"

Yogurt is a relatively liquid food. You may be able to make a small pile of it, but over time, the pile will spread out. If you leave it out of the cold too long, you'll notice the yogurt begins to separate and liquefy. When you add cornstarch to the mixture, it absorbs some of that liquid, firming up the yogurt a bit but not enough to turn it into a solid. It remains **moldable** and pliable.

Devotional

Have you made your preposterous putty yet? Yes? Great! Here's what I want you to do with it. I want you to make a heart out of your putty. That's right! Ready? On your mark, get set, go!

Now I want you to say this out loud: "God made me and loves me!" Turn to someone else and say, "Hey, you! God made you and loves you!" Then turn to another person and say the same thing: "Hey, you! God made you and loves you!"

It's true! God made you and loves you. But you know what? Sometimes we forget that God made us and loves us.

I forgot that God made me once when I was in fifth grade. I decided to stay inside at recess one day because I was working really hard on this magnificent science experiment with five hundred bouncy balls, forty-seven bottles of glitter glue, and a dozen plus one bottles of shaving cream. I wanted to see what happened when bouncy balls were covered with glitter glue and then with shaving cream. Would the balls still bounce? I had to find out!

But some of the other kids in my class laughed at me. They said I was really weird for liking science instead of wanting to go outside for recess. But then I remembered something my mom always told me: "God made you and loves you!"

Sometimes we look at other people and start to believe things like: *Maybe I am really weird. Maybe if I were someone else, people would like me more.*

Well, here's what I say to that: theory incorrect! We have evidence from the Bible that says something completely different. In Isaiah 64:8, the prophet Isaiah says this: "And yet, O LORD, you are our Father. We are the clay, and you are the potter. We all are formed by your hand."

You might not have taken that long to make your putty heart, and maybe you made a mistake along the way. But God is a perfect Creator, and he never makes mistakes. In fact, later in the New Testament, the apostle Paul tells us more about how God made us.

In Ephesians 2:10, Paul writes: "We are God's masterpiece. He has created us anew in Christ Jesus, so we can do the good things he planned for us long ago." Do you know what a masterpiece is? It could be a perfect painting, a perfect sculpture, a perfect drawing—with no mistakes. A masterpiece is the most wondrous, marvelous, fizztastic thing ever!

And you are a masterpiece—made by God himself!

So next time you see a mirror, point at yourself and say, "God made you and loves you!"

Collecting Your Family's Data

What did you observe as you mixed the two ingredients together? Did you have to add more cornstarch or more yogurt to get the texture you wanted?

....

Describe the texture and shape of your preposterous putty.

....

What is something unique about you?

....

In what ways can you use your unique design for God?

....

Prayer Time

Take some time to thank God for creating your family. Thank him for as many things about each person as you can think of.

PIZZA BOX SOLAR OVEN

Fiery Furnace

(Daniel 3)

Introduction

Greetings! I hope you brought your appetite, because today's experiment involves food. First, we're going to need a pizza box, so call and order some pizza! But save room for dessert—after we use the pizza box to build a solar oven, we're going to test it out by making s'mores. It sounds like a delicious day ahead.

WARNING! This experiment requires a box cutter and heat. Safety first!

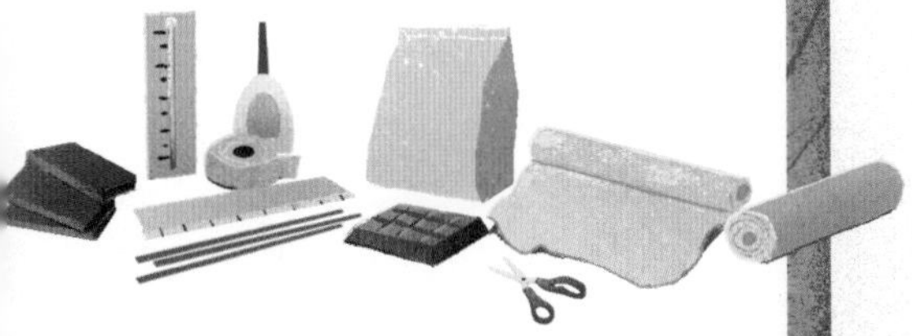

Fizzlebop Supply List

- Cardboard pizza box
- Aluminum foil
- Box cutter
- Duct tape
- Black plastic garbage bag
- Glue
- Clear kitchen plastic wrap
- Wooden kebab stick
- Thermometer
- Chocolate bars, marshmallows, and graham crackers for the s'mores
- Heat-safe plate

The Experiment

1 Open the pizza box and wrap the outside in aluminum foil to insulate it.

2 Use the box cutter to carefully cut a U shape into the top lid of the pizza box. Leave at least 1 inch (2.5 cm) between the sides and flap. This should create a flap that can bend upward when the pizza box is closed.

3 Cut out a sheet of aluminum foil that will cover your flap, but also be able to wrap around the sides of the flap by ½ inch (1.25 cm).

4 Wrap this aluminum foil around the inside of the flap so it faces downward into the pizza box.

5 Use the duct tape to secure the foil. The foil will act like a mirror, reflecting the sunlight.

6 Fold the black garbage bag into a square. The color black absorbs light, and light is energy, which creates heat.

7. Glue the plastic square to the bottom of the interior of the pizza box.

8. Under the flap, place plastic wrap across the opening in the top of the box and secure it with tape.

9. Support the aluminum-covered flap by poking the kebab stick into the lid of the pizza box and using it to prop up the flap.

   FIZZ TIP: Create a loop of tape at the edge of the flap. This will allow you to adjust the angle of the lid as the sun moves.

10. Put the thermometer on the black plastic square and record an initial temperature reading in the observations section below.

11. Place the pizza box oven in a sunny outside area and record the temperature within the pizza box every 20 minutes. Move the flap whenever necessary to keep the sun's rays reflecting off the foil on the underside of the flap.

12. Try to cook a s'more. Put a graham cracker on a heat-safe plate, stacking it with a piece of chocolate, a marshmallow, and a second graham cracker. Now set it in your solar oven and wait. Yummy!

"Dr. Fizzlebop, what's happening?"

Solar ovens work by trapping heat energy from the sun. In this experiment, you directed heat energy from the sun through the clear plastic film using the reflective aluminum foil flap. Once the pizza box captured the heat, the garbage bag absorbed the heat energy, and the air temperature within the pizza box oven rose. It rose high enough to not only melt the chocolate but soften the marshmallow as well.

Devotional

Do you know what Bible story this solar oven reminds me of? The story of Shadrach, Meshach, and Abednego! If you've read that story before, you might remember why King Nebuchadnezzar sent them to the fiery furnace. He decreed that all of his people should bow down to a gold statue at certain times, and any who refused would be thrown to the flames.

When I was in third grade, we studied the Roman Empire. As part of our grade, we were required to write a report about the major events during this period. When I got my paper back, I had a big C- written across the top in red ink. I'd never gotten a B before—most certainly not a C! Expeditiously (which means quickly), I scanned my paper to find where I'd gone wrong. A single sentence was underlined: "In AD 30, Jesus Christ, the Son of God, appeared before Pontius Pilate, who was the Roman governor of Judaea."

Before I could raise my hand, the bell rang and class was over. I stopped by Ms. Grumperton's desk and asked why it was wrong.

"This was not in our lesson, and consists of nonhistorical information," was her short answer.

"Excuse me, Ms. Grumperton, can you show me what is not factual?" I inquired.

She sighed, then pointed to the sentence underlined in red. "This is not true."

"But it is—it's in the Bible, and recorded in Roman history," I said. "I checked both sources."

She grunted. "I'll tell you what, Phineas. Remove these three words, and I will raise your grade back to an A. It will then be factual."

The words in question were "Son of God."

My answer was swift. "No. Jesus was the Son of God, and it is impossible and scientifically inaccurate to deny that."

"Then a C- it is, and that is generous. Now you need to go catch your bus," she said and waved her hand for me to leave.

I felt like Shadrach, Meshach, and Abednego. These three men knew in their hearts that they must not betray the one true God in this way. So they refused to bow. The king was furious when he learned of this. Read Daniel 3:16-18 to see how they responded to the king.

Whether God saved their lives or not, they knew they needed to obey him. They understood that bowing down to that idol would mean worshiping a false god. And I knew that changing my answer would be denying the truth. Though I wasn't facing a fiery furnace, I stood by my answer—and the C-.

God delivered the three men from the furnace. Because of their act of true faith, King Nebuchadnezzar declared that the God of Israel should be worshiped throughout all of Babylon.

The response to Shadrach, Meshach, and Abednego's courageous faith was quick, but sometimes we don't see the results of our actions until later. My grade wasn't changed. It was still a C-. But guess what? A couple years later when I was choosing a sprinkled doughnut from our church's coffee and doughnuts table, someone tapped me on the shoulder. I nearly jumped out of my dinosaur slip-ons—it was Ms. Grumperton, and she was in my church narthex (which is a neato word for lobby).

"Phineas, you were correct. Jesus was tried by the Roman governor Pontius Pilate," she said. Then she sighed softly. "I need to apologize. I borrowed a friend's Bible and read about the trial of Jesus. And then I kept reading and did some additional researching and cross-referencing." Her eyes filled with tears. "You were so resolute—" (which means unwavering)—"in your answer that it made me ponder my own beliefs. And as I analyzed the facts, as you put it, I came to the same conclusion as you. It took me two years, but your paper deserves an A+." Then she opened her Bible and pulled out a copy of my report. She had crossed out the C- and changed it to an A+.

And then she said something that changed my life forever. "Because of your unwavering faith, Jesus now lives in my heart."

So whenever anyone challenges my faith, or questions my belief in God and Jesus, I think about Ms. Grumperton and her decision to follow Jesus.

Take some time to read the full story of these brave men

in Daniel 3 and be encouraged to stand firm in your faith and knowledge of Jesus Christ as the Son of God.

Collecting Your Family's Data

Temperature	Time
Initial Temperature: _____	@ Time: _____
Second Temperature: _____	@ Time: _____
Third Temperature: _____	@ Time: _____
Fourth Temperature: _____	@ Time: _____
Fifth Temperature: _____	@ Time: _____
S'more Cooking Temperature: _____	@ Time: _____
Time It Took to Eat S'more:	_____ Seconds

Describe what you observed about the s'more inside the solar oven.

Have you ever had to stand up for what you believe? If so, what happened?

Why did Shadrach, Meshach, and Abednego decide to obey God even though they weren't sure if he would set them free from the furnace?

Prayer Time

Amazing Creator, give us the courage to stand strong in our faith.
Even in the face of adversity, may we declare that you are the one true
God. Give us the strength to risk everything for you. Amen.

INVISIBLE INK and DECODER

The Writing on the Wall

(Daniel 5)

Introduction

We're swapping our lab coat for sunglasses, a trench coat, and a hat. Have you ever pretended to be a spy, delivering and decoding secret messages? Today's experiment involves writing messages with invisible ink, and we'll learn about a man named Daniel, who was the only one able to decode messages from God for King Belshazzar. Are you intrigued (which means interested)? Here we go!

WARNING! This experiment requires heat. Safety first!

Fizzlebop Supply List

- A few drops of lemon juice
- 1 tbsp (15 mL) of water
- Spoon
- Mixing bowl
- Cotton swabs
- White paper
- Lamp (with incandescent light bulb)
- Bible

The Experiment

Mix the water and lemon juice in a bowl.

Dip a cotton swab into the mixture and write a message on a piece of paper. (I wrote "Psalm 119:11.")

Wait for the juice to dry. You'll know it's dry when you can no longer see it.

Now deliver your secret message to someone and tell the receiver to hold it close to a lamp. The secret ingredient here is *heat*.

FIZZ TIP: LED lights typically do not produce very much heat, so they may not work for this step. If you don't have a lamp with an incandescent bulb, try using a hair dryer.

Now decode my secret message: open your Bible to Psalm 119:11 and read it with your family.

141

"Dr. Fizzlebop, what's happening?"

Lemon juice is made of **organic** material. Adding the water thins the lemon juice, making it nearly impossible to see. But when you add a little heat, the carbon compounds in the lemon juice break down, releasing the carbon. The carbon then **oxidizes** (which occurs when it encounters air), turning brown and revealing the message.

Devotional

Believe it or not, becoming a scientist wasn't my only dream—and neither was becoming an archaeologist, a paleontologist, or an aerospace engineer. I *also* imagined myself as a secret spy traveling the world. But then I realized part of the appeal of becoming a spy was all the cool gadgets. And the more I got into the science behind spy gadgets—from invisible ink to high-flying drones—the more fascinated I became. I found it wasn't the spies' work but how they could do their work that interested me.

When you give a secret message to a friend, he or she may not realize a message exists on the paper. You know the secret to decoding the blank paper, and your friend needs you to provide them with that information.

God used his servant Daniel to decode a message for the king. Daniel was the only one in all of Babylon who could interpret the writing on the wall. That's because he knew how to communicate with God and listen for his meaning. Turn in your Bible to Daniel 5 and read the whole story with your family.

Unlike the message that you wrote with invisible ink, the message Daniel communicated to Belshazzar wasn't pleasant. But the message was from God, and so Daniel had to share it.

Someday God might put you in a position to speak the truth to someone who needs it—maybe even someone who doesn't know God's love and care. He may allow you to help someone make sense of a situation in their life by using his words in the Bible. The Bible is kind of like a decoder: it provides insight into God's story and direction for our lives, and it gives us hope when we are worried. The more time we spend reading the Bible and praying, the easier it is to understand God's plan—and to talk about him with others.

Collecting Your Family's Data

What was it like watching your message dry and become invisible?

....

Can you think of any other liquids that might work in place of lemon juice?

....

Have you ever shared the truth about Jesus with someone else? If yes, what did you say? If not, how can you prepare to do this in the future?

....

Prayer Time

Take a moment to ask God for his boldness in your life—that you may be able to share about him with those around you. Ask God to put on your heart the name of someone who needs to hear about his love.

FUNNELPHONE

Jonah and the Big Fish
(Book of Jonah)

Introduction

Have you ever listened to a recording of wondrous whale sounds? At first, whale noises sounded a bit eerie (which means scary) to me, but the longer I listened, the more I began to hear something calming and beautiful. Did you know that whales are very intelligent and have their own language? They don't need telephones or computers to communicate from far away—the water in which they live transfers sound over great distances. In today's experiment, we're going to learn about underwater sound, while the devotional will take us to a story about an underwater call to God. Let's bop!

WARNING! This experiment requires scissors and a bathtub of water. Safety first!

Fizzlebop Supply List

- Scissors
- Balloon
- Small plastic funnel
- 4 ft (1.2 m) of rubber tubing (wide enough to fit over the smaller opening of both funnels)

FIZZ TIP: Look for tubing in the plumbing section of your local hardware store.

- Medium plastic funnel
- Duct tape
- Your bathtub, filled halfway with water
- Family member
- 5 of each of these items: marbles, nickels, wooden blocks (that can get wet), carrots

The Experiment

Cut off and discard the first ½ in (1.25 cm) of the balloon's opening.

Stretch the remaining portion of the balloon over the wide end of the smaller funnel.

FIZZ TIP: Make sure the balloon is tightly stretched across the funnel.

Fit the open ends of the rubber tubing over each of the narrow ends of the 2 funnels.

FIZZ TIP: Secure the connections of the tube and funnels with tape if necessary.

Place the funnel covered with the balloon into the water in the bathtub.

5 Place the other funnel over your ear and listen.

6 Ask a family member to roll the marbles down the side of the bathtub one at a time. Describe what you hear in the spaces below.

7 Ask a family member to drop the nickels in the water one at a time. Describe what you hear. Repeat this step with the wooden blocks and the carrots.

8 Have a family member put their face into the water and talk. Describe what you hear.

"Dr. Fizzlebop, what's happening?"

Sounds are produced by vibrations. By stretching the balloon over one end of the funnel, you created a surface to **amplify** the vibrations that were caused when the objects were dropped into the water. That sound traveled up the tubing to the other funnel. Sound travels farther and faster through water than it does through the air because liquid molecules are packed more tightly together than gas molecules.

FIZZ TIP: If you have access to a pool, try your funnelphone there as a family.

Devotional

Oh! I'm glad you're back! I was just out visiting my good friend Dr. Swishpop's fishpond. It's in her backyard, and she keeps lots of amazing fish there in all kinds of sizes and colors. It was fizztastic!

Speaking of fish, let's dive in to a story in the Bible that features a really big fish! You see, there was this guy named Jonah, and God gave him a special mission: God wanted

Jonah to go to a city called Nineveh and tell the people there about God.

But that is exactly what Jonah did *not* want to do. In fact, instead of going to talk to the people in Nineveh, Jonah ran away! He hurried down to the docks and got on a boat headed in the opposite direction.

You see, Jonah didn't want to tell the people in Nineveh about God because those people had actually sent an army to attack Israel, where Jonah lived. Jonah didn't think God should forgive them for their sins.

Once Jonah was on the boat, God sent a huge storm that almost broke up the entire ship. Jonah realized that God sent that storm because of him, so he told the captain to throw him overboard. As soon as Jonah was thrown in the sea, the storm stopped, and God sent a huge fish to swallow Jonah whole.

Open your Bible to Jonah chapter 2. Read what happened to Jonah inside the fish, and then meet me back here.

Finished reading? Isn't that amazing? God heard Jonah even though Jonah was underwater, inside a huge fish. In today's experiment, we created our very own underwater phone. When we listened through the funnelphone, we were able to hear the sounds of falling marbles and blocks so much better!

Here's the amazing truth: God hears us no matter where we are. We could be in a submarine underwater exploring the depths of God's creation or in a space station watching the stars go by. Even when we're in the middle of trouble like Jonah, God hears us.

Think about your own life. What is something you need to talk to God about today? Maybe something's bothering you or you feel stuck. Or maybe you're really excited about something stupendous. Tell God all about it!

Collecting Your Family's Data

Describe what you heard when the following items were dropped into the bathtub.

Marbles:

....

Nickels:

....

Wooden blocks:

....

Carrots:

....

Could you understand what was said when someone talked into the water?

....

Have you ever wondered if God was listening to you? If yes, why were you unsure?

....

Prayer Time

Amazing Creator, thank you for always hearing us, no matter where we are and no matter what's happening! You really are a magnificent, wondrous, and amazing Creator. Amen.

ICE FISHING

Fishing for People

(Matthew 4:18-22)

Introduction

Don't worry—you won't need your winter parka, gloves, or hat for this experiment. It isn't the sort of ice fishing where you sit around a hole in the ice searching for Old Grundy. In fact, we won't even be concerned with fish. We're actually going to be catching ice cubes on our line today!

FIZZ FACT: Old Grundy is a reference to one of Dr. Fizzlebop's favorite *Adventures in Odyssey* episodes, "Ice Fishing."

Fizzlebop Supply List

- 12 in (30 cm) string
- Popsicle stick
- Tape
- 3 cups (720 mL) water
- Glass mixing bowl (one that's big enough to hold the water)
- Ice cubes
- 1 tsp (5 g) salt
- 1 tsp (5 g) sugar
- 1 tsp (5 g) flour

The Experiment

1. Build your fishing pole by tying the string to the Popsicle stick. Use a piece of tape to secure the string to the stick.

2. Pour the water into the mixing bowl, then add the ice cubes to the bowl. They should float at the surface.

3. Set one end of the string from the fishing pole on top of an ice cube. Sprinkle salt over the spot where the string and ice cube touch. Wait about 10 seconds and slowly pull up on the fishing pole. Observe and record what happens.

4. Repeat step 3 with one of the other ice cubes, but this time use sugar instead of salt.

5. Repeat step 3 with the final ice cube, but this time use flour instead of salt.

"Dr. Fizzlebop, what's happening?"

Water typically freezes at 32°F (0°C). By adding salt to the water, we lowered the water's freezing point, meaning it had to get even colder to freeze. (Sugar and flour don't share this property with salt, so they don't work the same way.) But as the ice melted, water was released, which increased the freezing point of the tiny pool on the surface of the ice cube. Once the freezing point rose, the pool of water refroze, trapping the string inside the ice.

Devotional

I love visiting aquariums. An aquarium is a building with giant fish tanks where tons of fish swim around and stare back at you through the glass. In fact, there's a magnificent aquarium near my house! I've visited it several times because I love seeing all the colors and shapes and sizes of the fish God created. He really is a marvelous Creator with such wondrous ideas.

Do you have a favorite kind of fish? Maybe it's a green one or a large one with lots of teeth—yikes!—or maybe it's a goldfish you have as a pet. Which I don't really think of as gold, but orange. Anyhow.

Did you know that some of Jesus' first followers were fishermen? They went out onto the Sea of Galilee all night long with nets, hoping to catch some fish to sell the next day. Well, one day, Jesus found those fishermen. Why don't you read all about it in Matthew 4:18-22, and then come back to this devotional?

Finished? Did you notice how Jesus said something fizztastic to Peter and Andrew on their boat? "Come, follow me, and I will show you how to fish for people!" Wait a second. What did Jesus mean?

Jesus wasn't saying that they would be sneaking around with fishing nets and throwing them over people. No! He meant that his followers would tell others about Jesus and all that he did for them.

And Jesus *did* do so much for us! Jesus is 100 percent God and 100 percent a human being. He showed us how to love God and love others perfectly, and then he died on a cross so he could defeat sin and death. Three days later, Jesus came back to life, and now anyone who decides to follow Jesus can become part of God's family forever!

But Jesus doesn't want only a few people to be part of his family. He extends this invitation to everyone! And that's where we come in. Jesus has sent us to tell others about him so lots and lots of people can decide to follow Jesus and join God's family too! That's awfully nifty if I do say so myself.

Today, think about this: Who can you tell about Jesus? Who can you share the love of God with?

Collecting Your Family's Data

Ingredients	What happened when you sprinkled the ingredient on the ice?	What happened when you pulled up on the fishing pole?
Salt		
Sugar		
Flour		

Why do you think certain ingredients worked while others did not?

What would it look like for you to be a fisher for people?

Have a family discussion about some ways you can share the news of what Jesus did for you. What ideas did you come up with?

....

Prayer Time

Amazing Creator, lead us to someone who needs to hear about you today. Give us the courage to share all that you have done. We pray that they would decide to follow you and become part of your family. Amen.

MAKING a BEE HOME

The Beatitudes

(Matthew 5:3-12)

Introduction

You may not realize it, but you've been experiencing the stupendous benefits of bees all your life. From the trees and flowers growing outside your home to the fruits and vegetables you eat, bees have been involved in helping them to grow—and grow abundantly. But have you ever said thank you? I suppose I haven't either, at least not in a way they could understand. Hey, perhaps that's an idea for a future invention—B-Phone or B-Talk . . . The name might need some work as well as the science. In the meantime, I thought we could show our exuberant appreciation by building a home for bees. Interested?

WARNING! This experiment requires scissors. Safety first!

Fizzlebop Supply List

- Paper straws (or construction paper, penc and masking tape)

  FIZZ TIP: Don't use plastic straws.

- Scissors
- Empty cardboard milk or juice carton
- Measuring tape
- Duct tape (variety of colors)
- 3 12-in (30 cm) zip ties
- Variety of colorful stickers

The Experiment

1. If you are using construction paper instead of paper straws, create the bee tubes by rolling the construction paper around the pencil. Use a piece of tape to keep the tubes from unrolling.

2. Cut off the top of the carton, creating an open square.

3. Measure the height of the carton. Then cut the construction paper tubes or paper straws to be slightly shorter than the carton's height.

4. Wrap the colorful duct tape around the outside of the carton to create a layer of protection from the weather. Add stickers for the finishing touch!

5. Fill the carton with the bee tubes, facing upward so the openings are accessible to the bees.

   FIZZ TIP: Be careful not to bend any of the tubes, but make sure the carton is tightly packed. None of the tubes should fall out if you turn the carton upside down.

6. Find a tree branch where you can secure your bee home.

   FIZZ TIP: Look for a spot that's secluded—not in an area where your family is usually active.

7. Wrap the zip ties around the bee home to secure it to the tree branch. These zip ties will keep it steady.

8. Over the next month, observe from a distance to see whether any bees have taken up residence.

"Dr. Fizzlebop, what's happening?"

Though our focus today was not an experiment but a service project, there is a bit of science involved in the packing of the carton. We didn't use tape or glue to hold the bee tubes in place—we only needed pressure and friction. The tighter we packed the tubes, the more pressure was exerted between and among the tubes, holding them in place. Friction between the tubes and the carton also helped to hold them in place.

FIZZ FACT: From the day honeybees are born, they zealously labor to pollinate as many flowers as they can. Did you know that every pound of honey the honeybees make represents over 2.6 million flowers pollinated? The honeybees in a hive will have traveled a distance equivalent to more than two times around the world to make that delicious treat. God designed honeybees to help our wondrous world have enough food to sustain life on planet Earth. In fact, honeybees do so much for our world that one in every three bites of food that you eat comes from a honeybee.

Devotional

I think we can all agree that the humble honeybee is a great model of a true servant. And bees are happiest when they are doing the work God designed them for. It's amazing how much impact a joyful servant's heart can have on the entire world.

Now, who else comes to mind when you think of a selfless and joyful servant like that? Jesus, of course! So it really is no surprise that Jesus preached about this very topic.

Have you ever heard of the Sermon on the Mount? In Matthew 5:3-12, Jesus preached to a multitude (which means a whole lot) of people. This passage in the Bible is known as the Beatitudes (which is a list of blessings spoken by Jesus). Sensing a little tie between the experiments and our devotional—BEE-atitudes? Sometimes I can't help myself. Can you guess what the Beatitudes are all about?

As you read the passage, you'll find that all eight Beatitudes describe a joy-filled servant. Jesus starts each one with the phrase "blessed are"—and in this context, *blessed* really means "joyful" or "happy." There's a promise, a challenge, and a reward wrapped up in each one. Let's take a quick look at all eight of them.

1. **Bee joyful** when you are *poor in spirit*, because you will find that *your riches are in God's Kingdom.*

2. **Bee joyful** when you *feel you have lost what is most precious to you*, because you will find *the deep love of the one who is truly most precious.*

3. **Bee joyful** with *however little you have*, because you will find *the Lord is the one who provides everything you truly need.*

4. **Bee joyful** when you are *hungry for righteousness*, because you will be *satisfied.*

5. **Bee joyful** when you *care for others*, because you will find that *you have a heavenly Father who cares for you.*

6. **Bee joyful** when *your heart is right with God,* because you will find that *God is at work in the world around you.*

7. **Bee joyful** by *helping others get along,* because you will find *the peace that comes from being part of the family of God.*

8. **Bee joyful** even when *others treat you badly* because you followed God's example, because *your golden reward—* your honey that lasts forever—*will be great in heaven.*

Being a joyful and selfless servant isn't always easy, but the good news is that when the Spirit lives in us, he is able to change our hearts.

And so today as we think about some of God's most selfless servants, **bee joyful** that he has designed the amazing world in which you live—from the bee to the bison to the tadpole to the tiger. They've all got a place in this amazing world, and so do you!

Collecting Your Family's Data

Describe the location you chose to hang your bee home. Why do you think it appeals to bees?

Record the first day you noticed bees moving into the bee home.

Are there any Beatitudes that require some extra effort for you?

What are some ways you can use the Beatitudes in your daily life?

Prayer Time

Take a minute today to thank Jesus, the Magnificent Son, for being the perfect servant. Ask him to change your heart into that of a joyful servant so you can bless the world and spread his joy just like the honeybee spreads pollen and helps plants grow. Be sure to thank God for the honeybee, too!

QUICKSAND

Building Your House on the Rock
(Matthew 7:24-27)

Introduction

Imagine with me for a minute that we are walking through a thick jungle in our boots and khakis. We're on the path to discovering a fascinating new slug, believed to only live in this part of the wilderness. Suddenly you hold up an arm and stop me. "What's wrong?" I ask, and you point to a mysteriously open spot ahead of us where nothing grows. "It's quicksand," you say. Thankfully you recognized the hazard, so we skirt (which means go around) the quicksand and continue on to discover the unique slug, which we name by combining the first three letters of your first name with the last three letters of my last name. And in honor of our imaginary adventure, today at Fizzlebop Labs we're going to look into the unique properties of quicksand by making some of our own.

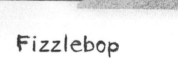

Fizzlebop Supply List

- 1 cup (120 g) cornstarch
- 1/2 cup (120 mL) water
- Glass mixing bowl
- Spoon
- Plate

The Experiment

1. Mix the cornstarch and water in the glass bowl.

2. Observe and record what happens when you stir it quickly versus when you stir it slowly.

3. Observe and record what happens when you poke it with a spoon or press on it hard with your hands.

4. Observe and record what happens when you scoop it up with a spoon and drip it onto a plate.

FIZZ TIP: You can store this mixture if you want to. But always stir the quicksand right before you use it.

CORN STARCH

"Dr. Fizzlebop, what's happening?"

Quicksand appears to be liquid, but when you push on it, it becomes firm under pressure. When the cornstarch grains are stirred quickly, they have difficulty sliding over each other due to the lack of water between them. When you stir them slowly, more water can get between the grains, and they slide over each other more easily. The same happens with poking. If you poke quickly, the substance becomes very hard. If you poke slowly, it remains runny.

Devotional

Imagine you're a grown-up, and you get to design a house and have it built exactly how you want it. What would you include in your house? Where would you build it? In your hometown? By the beach? In the mountains? By a lake? Would it be a cottage, a tree house, a castle?

No matter where you build, one thing is extremely important: the foundation. What do you think would happen if you built a house right on top of a sandy beach? Open your Bible to Matthew 7:24-27 to see if you guessed it.

So how do we make sure our house is built on solid rock? If you were building at the beach, you'd need to drill down into the bedrock beneath the sand and anchor the house to that deep, firm foundation.

But what about our lives? How do we make sure we're building on rock instead of sand? Hmmm . . . if sand represents things that change and shift and collapse in life, what are some examples of those?

Perhaps you've gone through a big change, such as who you hang out with or where you live. If you've ever moved or gone to a new school, you know what that's like.

Perhaps a grandparent or someone close to you has died. Perhaps one of your friendships has ended. Whether your loss has been great or small, you know how hard it was. Sometimes our lives change dramatically, and we may feel as if our whole world is being shaken.

But would you like to know a wonderful secret? It's found in one of my favoritest verses, Isaiah 54:10. "'For the mountains may move and the hills disappear, but even then my faithful love for you will remain. My covenant of blessing will never be broken,' says the LORD, who has mercy on you."

Did you catch that? Even if the entire landscape changes, God's faithful love for you will remain! His marvelous, never-ending, steadfast love for you is as solid as a rock and is a firm foundation on which you can build your entire life. His love is also a safe place to put your hope! Of all the things in this world, nothing is as steadfast or as dependable as God's great love for you. Count on it!

Collecting Your Family's Data

Describe the quicksand when you stirred it quickly versus when you stirred it slowly.

....

Describe what happened when you poked it with a spoon or pressed on it hard with your hands.

....

Describe what happened when you scooped it up with a spoon and dripped it onto a plate.

....

What's the biggest change you've gone through in your life? How did it affect you?

....

When it feels like your world is being shaken, how can you hold on to God's great love?

....

Prayer Time

Amazing Creator, thank you for your steadfast, unshakable love. Help each of us to put our trust in you and only you—and to build our lives on your firm foundation. Amen.

SINK or FLOAT

Jesus Walks on Water
(Matthew 14:22-33)

Introduction

Have you ever wondered what it would be like to walk on water? Ever since I read about Jesus doing it in the Bible, I've wanted to see if there was a way I could do it. I've tried everything—from the simple "step out onto the surface of a lake from a dock" method to the "getting a running head start" method (speed being the key), to the "tying kickboards to my feet" method. And I have considered those inflatable clear balls you can get inside and roll around in on the water. But then my claustrophobia (fear of enclosed spaces) kicks in and I just can't. Today, however, we're going to perform an experiment that demonstrates flotation. This one is super-simple, but the concept of how and why is neato.

Fizzlebop Supply List

- Large mixing bowl
- Water (enough to nearly fill the bowl)
- Orange

The Experiment

1. Pour the water in the mixing bowl.

2. Put the orange in the water and observe.

3. Remove the orange and peel the rind. Set the rind aside.

4. Put the orange back in the water and observe. Then put the rind in the water and observe. Record your observations.

"Dr. Fizzlebop, what's happening?"

When you first put the orange in the bowl of water, it floated, right? And then when you peeled off the rind, it sank. Why? Well, take a look at the orange rind. It's covered in tiny divots, which act as air pockets. This air gives the orange a lower density than water, allowing it to float. When you remove the rind (and thereby the air pockets) from the orange, its density increases, making it sink.

Devotional

Today's experiment reminds us that sometimes the smallest of changes can yield dramatically different results. When you removed the skin of the orange, it sank quickly, but with the skin on, the orange could float safely on top of the water. Keep this in mind as you read today's Bible passage, Matthew 14:22-33.

Jesus must have known what would happen when Peter asked if he could walk on the water too, but he still called Peter to come. It was time for Peter (and us) to learn a lesson.

I can just imagine Peter's slightly nervous but enthusiastic grin as he put his feet out of the boat and onto the water. He didn't sink! The disciples in the boat must have been going crazy!

One marvelous step.

Two more wondrous steps.

While the first few steps seemed to be going stupendously for Peter, the focus of his heart shifted. Instead of trusting Jesus to keep him afloat, Peter got distracted by the sweeping wind and rolling waves surrounding him. When he took his sight off Jesus, he began to sink.

Jesus immediately reached out to save Peter and said to him, "You have so little faith. Why did you doubt me?"

Just like the orange in our experiment, something changed in Peter from the time he had his "skin" on to when he lost it. With its skin, the orange stays afloat. Without it, the orange will sink every time. Peter's faith that Jesus was keeping him afloat was his "orange skin."

Often, as much as we *want* to be like Jesus, we find ourselves falling short of the goal. We get so distracted and scared of what might be happening around us that we fail to realize that Jesus is there to keep us from sinking.

Next time your life gets a little stormy, remember this orange experiment. Keep your faith in Jesus and you'll be able to walk safely through any storm. And when you fail like Peter did, Jesus will be right there to catch you. So go boldly, and know that the Son of God has you firmly in his magnificent grip.

Collecting Your Family's Data

What happened when you first put the orange in the water?

....

What happened when you put the peeled orange in the water?

....

What happened when you put the rind in the water?

....

What do you need to trust Jesus with today?

....

Prayer Time

Jesus, help us to trust you with everything we are. Even when the storms billow around us, remind us that you are in control. Amen.

COLORFUL KALEIDOSCOPE

The Great Commission
(Matthew 28:19-20)

Introduction

It's obvious (which means clear and simple) that we are ecstatic about color here at Fizzlebop Labs. You'll find it in many of the experiments we conduct. Imagine if our world were all gray. It would be so boring! But God isn't boring—he's fizztastic—so he created a world with limitless colors. Ponder (which means think about) this idea: knowing God is kind of like being full of color. If you have friends who don't know God, it's like their lives are gray. When you tell them about God and they trust in him, they become colorful, exuberantly filled with his love. Now imagine God's love spreading through a dark and gray world, and the world becoming full of joy and color. Kind of a neato image, right? Today's experiment might just make this visual come to life.

Fizzlebop Supply List

- 2 cups (480 mL) whole milk

  FIZZ TIP: Low-fat milk does not work.

- Baking sheet with sides
- Food coloring (3 different colors)
- Liquid dish soap

The Experiment

1. Slowly pour the milk onto the baking sheet so a thin layer covers the bottom. Cover the whole baking sheet.

2. At different locations on the sheet, add 8 drops of food coloring onto the milk. Use all 3 colors for the best effect!

3. Add 5 drops of liquid dish soap onto the food coloring and observe.

4. Discard the colored milk. Do not drink it.

"Dr. Fizzlebop, what's happening?"

Why did we use whole milk instead of skim milk? Well, the fat content in whole milk is higher, and that fat is what we needed. You see, dish soap is formulated to attack fat that is left on dirty dishes. In our experiment, though, the liquid dish soap was attacking the fat content in the whole milk. The dish soap actually dissolved the fat, and while it worked, it created a kaleidoscope of color for us to see.

Devotional

Do you know who created the beauty of color, like that kaleidoscope we just saw? Who formed the universe, spoke Earth into existence, and filled it with life, beauty, and unique design? Who created both the tiny ant and the giant giraffe? Who gave the ladybug its colorful coat and the zebra its stripes?

Who made some people tiny and some tall? Some with light skin and some with dark? Some with bright-red hair and some with shiny black locks? Why do you suppose God created plants, animals, and people in a variety of shapes, sizes, and colors?

When God sent his only Son into the world, he didn't send Jesus to die only for Jews, or Samaritans, or Jamaicans, or Americans, or Chinese, or Brazilians, or Germans, or Syrians, or Cubans. He sent Jesus for the salvation of the whole world. The whole world!

What does that mean for you and for me? Take a look at Jesus' words in Matthew 28:19-20. Jesus wants every person, from every nation, to have the opportunity to know God's love. He wants us to share what God has done for us. He also wants us to teach others how to obey God's commands, because they help us know the most fizztastic and satisfying way to live!

But you know what my favoritest part of this Scripture passage is? "Be sure of this: I am with you always, even to the end of the age."

Jesus doesn't send us out into the world alone. He is with us! That means we can talk with him anytime, just as you would talk to your closest friend.

When Jesus becomes your friend, he'll fill you with such joy and love, you'll find yourself loving everyone around you. That's when you'll be the very best ambassador of God to the world that you can possibly be. After all, you'll be introducing people to your best friend!

Collecting Your Family's Data

Describe the movement of the colors on the tray.

....

Do you think using a different soap would have affected the outcome? Give it a try!

....

Why do you think God created so much variety in the world?

....

What's something you've learned from someone who is different from you?

....

Prayer Time

Amazing Creator, we're filled with your colorful love! We want to share it with those who don't yet know you. Help us show them your exuberant colors so they may know you. Amen.

SOAP-POWERED BOAT

Jesus Calms the Storm
(Mark 4:35-41)

Introduction

Greetings! Have you ever been on a boat? Was it big or small? Were you on a lake, a river, or the ocean? Maybe your boat was powered by the wind or a diesel engine, or maybe by you with a paddle. Regardless, your boat required a force to make it move. Being on the boat also required faith—faith that it wouldn't sink. You believed that the boat would float, or you never would have boarded it! Our experiment and devotional are going to cover both of these swell topics.

WARNING! This experiment requires scissors. Safety first!

Fizzlebop Supply List

- Piece of sturdy non-corrugated cardboard, at least 6 x 6 in (15 x 15 cm)
- Scissors
- Baking sheet with sides
- Water (enough to nearly fill the baking sheet)
- 1 tsp (5 mL) liquid dish soap
- Toothpick

The Experiment

1 Cut the cardboard into a boat shape about 3 inches (8 cm) long and 2 inches (5 cm) wide.

FIZZ TIP: Cut a point at the front and leave the sides and back straight.

2 Cut a triangle-shaped notch into the back of the boat, with one point of the notch facing away from the boat. The sides of the notch should be about ½ inch (1.25 cm) each.

3 Fill the baking sheet with water. The water should just meet the rim of the baking sheet.

4 Dip the toothpick into the liquid dish soap and use it to dab the soap onto the sides of the notch.

5 Carefully place the boat on the surface of the water and observe.

FIZZ TIP: You can repeat the experiment until the cardboard becomes too soggy, but make sure to empty your tray, rinse it very well, and use fresh water each time.

"Dr. Fizzlebop, what's happening?"

The dish soap you are using is a type of **surfactant**. That sounds like a big word, but all it means is the soap breaks the surface tension of the water. When the surface tension is broken, force is created. Because the boat is lightweight, this force is just enough to send it sailing across the baking-sheet sea. Neato!

Devotional

I think we can all agree that life gets a little out of control at times. The funny thing is, it often doesn't take a big event to set our hearts and minds into panic mode. Sometimes it's just the simplest things.

1. Your phone breaks.
2. You have trouble with a friend.
3. An experiment stains your lab coat.

The problems on that list may seem like trivialities (which means minor things), but because we often have no control over them, they can cause our whole day to go sideways. And if I'm honest, some of the smallest blunders I've made have felt ridiculously important in the moment. And then there are those big disasters that can send our lives into a tailspin.

Here's the thing. When you find yourself in a chaotic moment—big or small—it's encouraging to know you aren't alone and that there is someone who is always in control.

Get out your Bible and read Mark 4:35-41.

This must have been an awfully terrible storm. Several of the disciples were veteran (which means experienced) fishermen and had probably handled some tough storms in their day. So we're not just talking about sprinkles on your windshield here. I'm guessing the waves were splashing up and over the sides of the boat and the wind was driving them sideways, twisting and turning. If there had been meteorologists in those days, they'd probably be telling everyone to take shelter immediately.

Thankfully for the disciples, there was someone in their boat who was not worried one bit. He was always in control, no matter what happened.

Do you know who that was? Jesus, of course!

He stood up and rebuked the wind and said, "Silence! Be still!"

Instantly the wind ceased, and there was a great calm.

But it's what he said to the disciples next that is most important for all of us to remember.

He looked them straight in the eyes and asked, "Why are you afraid? Do you still have no faith?"

God knows we're going to have big and small problems that are out of our control. He knows that life will give us hurricanes and rainstorms. The important thing to remember is that when the storms do come, no matter their size, we aren't alone in the boat. Jesus has the power to overcome any storm.

Collecting Your Family's Data

How far did your boat sail across the baking sheet?

....

How do you think you could improve your boat (materials or design)?

....

Think of a life event that seemed overwhelming at the time. What did you do?

....

How might trusting God help you navigate the toughest moments?

....

Prayer Time

Take a moment to pray for each other by name. Ask God to strengthen everyone's faith so that it is strong and resolute (which means solid) when life brings small or big trials.

LEVITATION

Jesus Returns in the Clouds
(Mark 13:26)

Introduction

As a young scientist, I always wondered what it would be like to walk on the clouds, the way I imagined angels did. Bouncing and soaring from an elephant-shaped cloud to a horse-shaped cloud—while avoiding the spider-shaped cloud! While neither you nor I will be flying today, I am ecstatic about our experiment. We are going to make an orb **levitate** (which means float in the air)! You may not believe your eyes when you see this. It's wondrous!

WARNING! This experiment requires scissors. Safety first!

Fizzlebop Supply List:

- Scissors
- Mylar tinsel for Christmas trees

  FIZZ TIP: Look for the thin nest and narrowest Mylar tinsel available.

- Balloon

The Experiment

Cut 6 strands of tinsel to about 6 inches (15 cm) each in length.

Tie the 6 strands together in a knot at both ends. This creates your orb.

Blow up the balloon and tie it.

Now create a charge by rubbing the balloon back and forth through your hair for 30 seconds. Then hold the balloon out in front of you.

With your free hand, hold the orb (by one of the knots) above the balloon.

6 Let the orb drop and touch the balloon.

7 The orb should repel away and start floating. Make sure to recharge the balloon between each levitation attempt.

FIZZ TIP: If the tinsel orb sticks to the balloon, the tinsel is probably too thick. Pull off one or more strands and try it again.

"Dr. Fizzlebop, what's happening?"

When you rubbed the balloon across your hair, you created a negative static charge across the balloon. The negatively charged electrons on the balloon attract the positively charged protons within the neutral orb. This stops when the negative charge on the balloon repels the negative charges within the orb. If the two are allowed to touch, some of the electrons from the balloon are transferred to the orb. This causes both the balloon and the orb to have a negative charge, which makes them repel each other. Like charges repel; opposite charges attract.

Devotional

Jesus sure showed us a lot of magnificent miracles during his time here on earth. He made a lot of promises too. Today we're going to talk about one promise that has yet to come true.

But first, let's recap just a few things that Jesus has already shown us he can do for us.

1. He fulfilled every prophecy about when and where the Messiah would be born.

2. He turned water into wine.

3. He helped fishermen catch more fish than they had ever seen.

4. He healed the blind, the lame, and the sick.

5. He raised the dead to life again.

6. He cast out demons.

7. He fed thousands with only a small amount of bread and fish.

8. He walked on water.

9. He calmed the wind and the waves.

10. He predicted his own death and willingly died for our sins.

11. He conquered the grave and rose from the dead himself.

12. He walked through walls.

13. He promised and delivered the Holy Spirit to his disciples.

14. He flew up into the sky and disappeared into the clouds.

Wow . . . is there anything that Jesus *can't* do?

Spoiler alert: nope.

With a track record like this, I think it's pretty important to listen to him when he makes a promise. After all, he has already proved himself to be all-powerful, all-knowing, and always caring for those he loves.

In Mark 13:26, Jesus makes a very special promise to us. He tells us that he will return one day. The clouds will open, and he will descend to earth again just as he left it. How cool is that? Much more magnificent than our levitating orb project, I can guarantee you that.

Jesus promises he will come back to make the whole world right again. And I'm 100 percent sure that he is going to make good on that promise.

So how about you?

Are you ready for him to return? Have you placed your life into his hands?

The Bible promises that "if you declare with your mouth, 'Jesus is Lord,' and believe in your heart that God raised him from the dead, you will be saved" (Romans 10:9, NIV)!

When you make Jesus your Lord, it simply means that you ask him to forgive your sins and start to live for him. From that point on, your life will no longer be yours—it will belong to him. And that's great news, because if we've learned anything, it's that Jesus is all-powerful . . . and we humans are NOT!

Only Jesus has proven that he has the power to conquer sin and death. That is the most important miracle of all. I am so glad he has promised to save me from death.

How about you? Are you willing to trust Jesus with your whole life?

Collecting Your Family's Data

What did you observe about the orb before it touched the balloon?

What changed about its behavior after it touched the balloon?

Can you think of any other miracles Jesus performed that aren't listed above?

Do you trust Jesus with your whole life? Why or why not?

Prayer Time

Magnificent Son, thank you for fulfilling your promises. Thank you for showing us that we can trust you beyond the shadow of a doubt. Amen.

STAINED-GLASS CANDY

Telling Stories through Stained Glass

(Mark 16:15)

Introduction

My grandma was the secretary at a beautiful old church. It had tall, arched ceilings of thick wood beams, the walls were made of handlaid brick, and most marvelous of all were the stained-glass windows. When we'd visit, we'd sing hymns in the sanctuary as the Sunday morning light glowed through the windows, illuminating the imagery. As the organ played, the voices rose, and the light glittered in the stained glass, I could feel the presence of the Holy Spirit around us. Stained glass has always fascinated me with its ability to reflect beauty and light—and in some cases tell stories. Did you know that you can make stained glass with sugar? Today at Fizzlebop Labs we're going to combine the science of crystallization with the art of creating a colorful masterpiece that is also a delicious treat!

WARNING! This experiment requires high heat. Safety first!

Fizzlebop Supply List

- Baking sheet
- Parchment paper
- Nonstick cooking spray
- Saucepan
- 1 3/4 cups (350 g) granulated sugar
- 1/2 cup (120 mL) corn syrup
- 1 cup (240 mL) water
- 1/8 tsp (0.5 g) cream of tartar
- Spoon or spatula
- Candy thermometer
- Flavor extract (optional)
- Food coloring

183

The Experiment

1. Line a baking sheet with parchment paper and coat with non-stick cooking spray.

2. In the saucepan, combine sugar, corn syrup, water, and cream of tartar.

3. Slowly bring this mixture to a boil, starting with very low heat. Do not stir the mixture while it's boiling. You'll want it to get to 300°F (149°C). This could take up to 30 minutes. Measure the temperature with the cooking thermometer.

   FIZZ TIP: It is important that the mixture reach a boil slowly, or the sugar could become discolored.

4. Once the mixture is completely melted and clear, remove the saucepan from the stove.

   FIZZ TIP: Use a flavor extract to make your candy glass taste amazing. We used cotton candy here at Fizzlebop Labs!

5. Carefully pour the mixture onto the lined baking sheet.

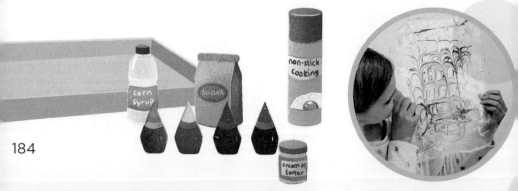

Spread the mixture with a spoon or spatula and let cool for 5 minutes. Add a few drops of food coloring and swirl them around to create a stained-glass look.

Now let the candy cool all the way until it is hardened.

When you're ready, shatter it and eat!

"Dr. Fizzlebop, what's happening?"

There are several similarities between making candy stained glass and real stained glass, but there are also big differences. For example, the temperature required for creating real glass is a whole heap hotter: you have to heat sand to over 3000°F (1649°C). When the sand cools, it forms what is called an **amorphous** solid. Amorphous solids are brittle (which means weak) and **transparent** (which means you can see through them).

Stained-glass sugar is created by dissolving sugar in water and heating it to 300–310°F (149–154°C). The temperature of the mixture and the sugar concentration rises as the water boils off. The sugar concentration in the syrup reaches about 99%.

If we did nothing else, we'd have what appears to be a clear piece of glass, but by adding in the food coloring and swirling it around, we created a marvelous work of art.

Devotional

If you still have some of your stained-glass candy—I understand if you don't, because trust me, I know how tasty it is—hold it up and let light shine through it. Does the color shine onto the floor or the wall? When light strikes stained glass, it illuminates (which means reveals) the colors and images for all to see and enjoy.

Have you ever visited a church with stained-glass windows? (Or maybe your own church has them!) What did you think of the colors, symbols, or pictures in the glass?

Many of the mosaics (which means colorful patterns) on stained-glass windows either tell a story or symbolize something significant. One of my favorite displays of stained glass had three segments. On the left was baby Jesus lying in the manger, surrounded by Mary and Joseph, as well as a few animals and an angel overhead. The center segment featured Jesus on the cross, his arms spread wide. In the final section to the right was Jesus clothed in white, with colorful rays coming out from his body. The birth, death, and resurrection of Jesus: God's plan to save his people, all in one display.

No words were used to communicate the story of Christ. But the vibrancy of the colorful glass as the sun shone through created a wondrous mosaic that spoke the zealous, magnificent love of God.

Hundreds of years ago, many people could not read or write, so handing someone a parchment or scroll (because books haven't always been around) was of no use. People often couldn't read or understand the words given to them. But the stories from the Bible could be communicated through pictures, too, and stained glass served as a way to share these wonderful stories with anyone who could see.

Mark 16:15 says, "Go into all the world and preach the Good News to everyone." How can we share the marvelous news of salvation with as many people as possible, so that they, too, might come to know Jesus in their hearts?

The world is full of ways to communicate, and I'm not only talking about the phone, television, radio, or social media. How might we communicate through art, like the stained glass of churches? We can communicate through songs, paintings, drawings, poetry, and so much more. God has made his people creative, and he has asked us to share the gospel. No one should be left out.

How will you do your part in reaching others? God has gifted you uniquely to reach someone, whether it's your neighbor, your friend, or people in the far reaches of the world. Use that gift for him, and go tell the Good News.

Collecting Your Family's Data

As you heated and stirred the sugar solution, what did you notice?

Describe what happened as you introduced color to the sugar solution.

What giftings has God given you to communicate creatively? How might you use those giftings to share the Good News?

Prayer Time

Encourage your family members during this time of prayer by acknowledging their giftings from God. Pray that God would use those gifts to grow his Kingdom.

CHICKEN SOUNDS
from a CUP

Peter's Denial of Jesus
(Luke 22:54-62)

Introduction

Have you ever heard a rooster crow or a chicken cluck? In today's experiment, we are going to replicate (which means copy) the sound of a chicken. Sound is a wondrous thing: it is invisible, yet impactful. You can't actually see sound, though you *can* see its effect on things or even feel it yourself. Some sounds are quiet and some are very loud, and today we're going to create an amplifier that will make the sound we produce louder and easier to hear. Are you ready?

WARNING! This experiment requires a nail. Safety first!

Fizzlebop Supply List

- Plastic drinking cup
- Nail
- 24 in (60 cm) yarn or cotton string

  FIZZ TIP: Nylon string does not work well.

- Paper clip
- Paper towels
- Water

The Experiment

1. Delicately punch a hole in the center of the bottom of the cup with the nail.

2. Tie one end of the yarn to the center of the paper clip.

3. Push the free end of the yarn through the hole in the cup and pull it through, leaving the paper clip on the outside of the bottom of the cup like an anchor.

4. Rip off a piece of paper towel about the size of a dollar bill, then fold it one time and get it damp in the water.
   FIZZ TIP: Do not soak the paper towel.

5. Holding the cup upside down, grip it tightly in one hand, then wrap the damp paper towel around the string near the cup.

6. Squeeze the string and pull down in short jerks so that the paper towel tightly slides along the string. Record what you hear.

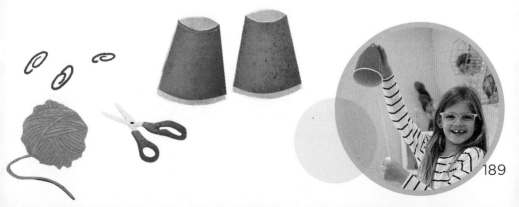

189

"Dr. Fizzlebop, what's happening?"

The vibrations from the string are nearly silent. However, when you add the cup, it amplifies the vibrations. Have you ever noticed the hole in an acoustic guitar? It's directly under the strings. This feature is called a sound hole, and it's used in guitars, mandolins, violins, lutes, and other instruments.

Devotional

Has anyone ever called you "chicken" because you didn't want to do something? What would you do if soldiers showed up to kidnap your best friend? Would you stay, or would you run and hide so the soldiers wouldn't take you, too?

After Jesus was arrested, Peter faced this very dilemma. Open your Bible and read Luke 22:54-62 to see what happened.

Peter was the only one of Jesus' disciples who dared to get out of the boat and walk on water! Peter had a big heart and a big mouth, which often got him in trouble. I'm a lot like Peter. I, too, am one to jump before I think. More than one experiment has gone awry (which means wrong) because I didn't take the time to ponder (which means think). Mostly, though, Peter's leaping to action because he trusted Jesus was a good thing. And yet Peter and I have something else in common too—something not so fizztastic.

This one kid in my class, Max, was really good at art—he could sculpt anything out of clay, and he made the best comic strips. They were so funny! One time my friends were making fun of one of Max's projects. I heard a voice in my head telling me this wasn't right, but I did nothing.

Then one of my friends tripped Max as he walked by. His clay sculpture fell and shattered into a gazillion pieces. A screw twisted in my stomach, and the voice inside me said this wasn't right. Yet again, I didn't listen—I said nothing.

Finally, as Max began to cry over the destruction of his

masterpiece, my friends started to laugh and point. And though my stomach churned and the voice sounded louder, I still did nothing. I just followed my friends as they walked down the hall and gave each other high-fives. I heard Max's whimpers behind me.

That night in my room, as I tried to pray, I began to cry. I realized how wrong I'd been. I hadn't acted as God had created me to act—in fact, like Peter, I'd denied Jesus three times. "I tell you the truth, Peter—this very night, before the rooster crows, you will deny three times that you even know me" (Matthew 26:34).

Three times the Spirit of God had prompted me to act, and three times I'd ignored him.

I knew what I had to do, so the next day I sought out (which means looked for) Max. He turned away as I approached, embarrassed. But I tapped him on the shoulder and said, "Max, I am very sorry." I told him that I was a Christian, but I hadn't acted like one. And that I was sorry for not standing up for him.

Instead of being angry or blowing me off, Max surprised me. He quoted my favorite Bible verse, Ephesians 4:32: "Be kind to each other, tenderhearted, forgiving one another, just as God through Christ has forgiven you." Max smiled. "I forgive you."

Relief washed over me, and that was a turning point in my life. It wasn't as though I never sinned again, but I knew that if I did, the best thing I could do was face the one I wronged and apologize.

And, you know, Peter changed too after Jesus forgave him. Peter became a man of action once again. This time, he would be sure his actions weren't based on his own ideas, but God's.

"Strengthen your brothers," Jesus told him (Luke 22:32). So that's what Peter did. He went on to become one of the greatest, most fizztastic leaders of Christ followers, with his weakness turned to marvelous strength. His story gave me hope then, and it gives me hope today. Is there someone in your life you've been unkind to? Or have you stood by while others were unkind to that person? Pray for God to give you the opportunity to not only seek forgiveness from them—but perhaps to even become friends.

Collecting Your Family's Data

Do you think the sound would be louder if you used a larger cup? Why or why not?

....

What other materials might you try rubbing on the string instead of a paper towel? Test them out and record the results below.

....

Think of a time you disobeyed Jesus and later asked for his forgiveness. How did it feel to be forgiven by him? Is there anything you need to ask forgiveness for right now?

....

Prayer Time

As a family, take a moment to pray for each other by name—that each of you would have the strength and courage to stand strong in your faith, even in the face of adversity (which means a challenge).

EGGSHELL GEODES

The Empty Tomb
(Luke 24:5-7)

Introduction

Welcome to the lab! We've got an eggcellent eggsperiment today. Did I say "eggcellent eggsperiment"? I meant "excellent experiment!" I've got eggs on my mind because today we are going to be using those intriguing white **ovoids**. Eggs are quite fragile, and you probably know that it's essential to be careful when handling them. In this experiment, however, we will be breaking a few shells and then taking what is broken and making something beautiful: eggshell **geodes**! Geodes are rocks with colorful minerals inside. These neato rocks are not only colorful but unique in how they develop.

WARNING! This experiment requires boiling water. Safety first!

Fizzlebop Supply List

- Saucepan
- 2 cups (480 mL) water
- Eggs (one for each geode you plan to make)
- Hot water
- Empty egg carton
- Heatproof measuring container that can hold the water
- 2 cups (500 g) sea salt or sugar
- Spoon
- Food coloring (pick your favorite color)

The Experiment

1. Start boiling the water in the saucepan.

2. While the water heats up, prepare the eggshells. Crack the eggs as close to the narrow end as you can. The more eggshell you have, the larger your geode will be.

   FIZZ TIP: Save the egg yolks and whites to make some delicious scrambled eggs.

3. Clean out the eggshells using hot water. The key is to remove the skin lining the inside of the shell. You can simply do this with your fingers, but be careful not to break the shell.

4. Place the clean eggshells in the empty egg carton with the openings facing up.

5. Once the water is boiling, pour it into the measuring container.

6. Now pour ½ cup (125 g) of your solid (sea salt or sugar) into the water.

7 | Stir the solid into the water until it dissolves.

8 | Add more of the solid into the water, a little at a time, until the mixture is entirely saturated (which means the solid will stop dissolving in the water).

9 | Add your choice of food coloring to the mixture and stir again. If you want to make different colors of crystals, portion the mixture into additional containers before adding the colors.

10 | Once the mixture is the color you like, pour it into the hollow eggshells. Fill the shells as full as possible, but do not allow them to overflow.

11 | Find a safe place to put your geodes and wait. Evaporation may take up to a few days, dependent on the humidity level of where your family lives.

"Dr. Fizzlebop, what's happening?"

Over the next several days, the water in the mixture will evaporate. As this takes place, the solid will re-form into colorful crystals on the eggshells' walls.

You've done it—you've made an eggshell geode! Wasn't that eggciting?

Devotional

Isn't it neato that we can create something so beautiful out of a broken eggshell?

Did you know that God can do the same thing with us? Sometimes it's easy to feel like we're not good enough or don't have the right skills for God to make something wondrous happen through us.

I know I've felt like that before. In grade school, I entered an experiment in the science fair. My colorful diorama was all set up in the school gymnasium, and my supplies sat ready for the experiment. The night before, the rabbit in the neighboring booth got loose and hopped onto my table, knocking over a beaker of water and a bowl of salt. The water saturated the salt and the bottom of my poster. Colors from my poster board drained onto the table and mixed with the spilled water and salt, creating a huge mess.

The next morning, I was exasperated (which means very frustrated) when I saw my table. What was I going to do? I needed to demonstrate evaporation, and here was a re-creation of the Dead Sea instead. That's when my mom had an idea. She asked the art teacher for a hair dryer.

When the judges came to my booth, I used the hair dryer to evaporate the water speedily. The salt crystals, now blue, began to reappear in marvelous formations. It looked like the inside of a crystal cavern. I ended up getting a gold star for creativity, and we all had a good laugh as a rainbow bunny hopped past, the result of my colorful mess.

What I saw as destruction—the death of my presentation—was the beginning of something new and better. I'm reminded of the Easter story in the Bible. Read all about it in Luke 24:5-7.

You see, though Jesus died on the Cross, there was something better coming. When he rose again, he defeated death. Death is done, and life is new.

I hope these eggshell geodes will remind you of growth and beauty. Because of what Jesus did on the Cross, the ugliness of sin and death can be washed away. We can have flourishing life in him!

Collecting Your Family's Data

Analyze and describe the eggshell geodes. What do you see (color, texture, shapes)?

....

How long did it take for the crystals to form?

....

How did it feel to take something broken and make it beautiful and new?

What are some things in your life (or your family's life) that you could ask God to make new?

Prayer Time

Take a moment to pray for each other and the things your family wants God to make new.

RAPID COLOR CHANGING

Water into Wine

(John 2:1-11)

Introduction

Greetings, and welcome to Fizzlebop Labs! Have you ever wondered how magicians do their tricks? I'll admit a few of their tricks are rather magnificent. Magicians' tricks are all illusions, of course, but many times real science is at work behind the scenes, whether mirrors and reflection, magnets and attraction, or something else. In today's experiment, there is some super-simple but neato science at work. And in the devotion we'll see Jesus perform an incredible miracle that might seem like science or magic, but it's actually an example of God's amazing power.

WARNING! This experiment requires iodine and hydrogen peroxide. Safety first! We also recommend reading the caution labels on each chemical.

Fizzlebop Supply List

- Safety goggles
- 3 16-oz (480 mL) jars
- Permanent marker
- 1 1000-mg or 2 500-mg vitamin C tablets
- Plastic bag
- Rolling pin
- 3/4 cup (180 mL) warm water
- Spoon
- Bottle of tincture of iodine (2%)
- Bottle of hydrogen peroxide (3%)
- Liquid laundry starch

  FIZZ TIP: If you can't find liquid laundry starch, substitute ½ tsp of cornstarch or potato starch.

The Experiment

1. Put on your safety goggles.

2. Line up the jars. Label the jars A, B, and C.

   FIZZ TIP: You can write directly on glass jars with a permanent marker and easily wash it off when you're done.

3. Put the vitamin C tablets into the plastic bag, and use the rolling pin to crush the tablets into powder (as fine as possible).

4. Pour all the powder, along with ¼ cup (60 mL) of warm water into Jar A. Stir for at least 30 seconds. This is now LIQUID A.

5. Put 1 tsp (5 mL) of LIQUID A, ¼ cup (60 mL) of warm water, and 1 tsp (5 mL) of iodine into Jar B. Observe and record what happens. Jar B now contains LIQUID B.

6. In Jar C, mix ¼ cup (60 mL) of warm water, 1 tbsp (15 mL) of hydrogen peroxide, and ½ tsp (2.5 mL) of the liquid starch. This is now LIQUID C.

7. Pour all of LIQUID B into LIQUID C. Observe and record what happens.

8. Pour the liquid back and forth between Jar C and Jar B four more times.

9. Set down the jar with the liquid in it and let it rest. Observe and record.

10. When finished, carefully pour all liquids down the drain with plenty of water and wash your hands.

"Dr. Fizzlebop, what's happening?"

You've just conducted a chemical reaction known as the iodine clock reaction. It is called a clock reaction because it takes a certain amount of time for the reaction to occur. You can adjust the amount of time it will take for the liquids to turn blue by changing the concentration of the reactants or the temperature. The blue color results when you form a starch-iodine complex. Vitamin C delays this reaction, but once the vitamin C is used up, the starch-iodine complex can form.

Devotional

Wow, we saw colored water become clear and then blue in our experiment! In today's Bible story, we're going to learn about clear water turning a deep red, as Jesus turns water into wine.

But Jesus isn't a magician or a scientist—he is the Son of God. There's no illusion to what Jesus did. The water really became wine—it didn't just change color like the water in our experiment.

Gather everyone together and read John 2:1-11.

A miracle, that's what we call it. Not an illusion, not an experiment. Not only does Jesus have access to amazing power through God, but he has unblinking faith in what his Father can do.

Making water into wine was as simple to Jesus as drinking a glass of water is to you. It was a natural extension of who he was, though it's unexplainable to us as humans. When you're the Son of the Creator, the Intelligent Designer of the whole universe, you have an in on how things work, from molecules to galaxies.

Fizzlebop Labs is a place where faith meets science. And as we ponder what it means for faith to meet science, you and I will begin to see how God carefully designed the world to function—and we'll come to understand that science is how we explain it.

Collecting Your Family's Data

Describe what happened when you put Liquid A into Jar B and added the iodine.

Describe what happened when you combined Liquid B and Liquid C.

Describe what happened when you allowed your final solution time to rest.

Have you ever experienced something that couldn't be explained?

Which miracle that Jesus performed do you find most intriguing?

....

Prayer Time

Amazing Creator, you've made the entire universe, from ants to galaxies. Miracles exist because you have chosen to perform them in this world. Help us to have a strong faith so we might see your hand in every aspect of the world around us. Amen.

STICK-FIGURE DANCE

Jesus Heals a Lame Man
(John 5:1-15)

Introduction

Have you ever made a flip-book with a stack of paper? I have! In my flip-books, I've drawn airplanes that take off and fly through the sky and cars that drive up and over hills and make cool jumps. Flip-books require lots of nearly identical drawings to bring an image to life while the pages flip past rapidly. But what if you could use water to make your drawing move? Today you're going to raise a stick figure off the surface on which it was drawn and give it movement, and you're going to discover a fantastic connection to our Bible story too.

Fizzlebop Supply List

- Glass pie plate
- Dry-erase marker (black, blue, or purple)
- Water

The Experiment

1 Draw a simple picture on the flat surface of the pie plate.

FIZZ TIP: A stick figure is a good one to start with.

2 Pour water into the pie plate slowly. Observe and record what is happening.

FIZZ TIP: Don't pour directly onto the drawing.

3 Swirl the water around. Shift the pie plate left, then right. Observe and record what you see.

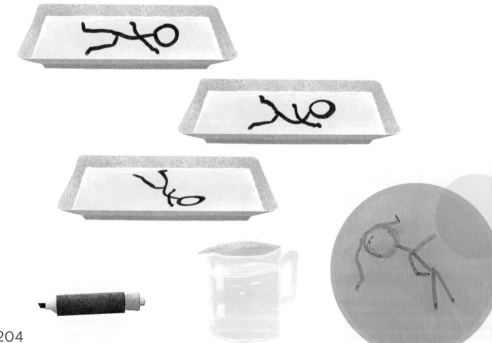

"Dr. Fizzlebop, what's happening?"

The dry-erase marker leaves behind a mixture of pigments and alcohol. The alcohol dissolves as the water is added, and the pigments are left behind as a solid. The glass pie plate is smooth, so the marker pigments slide right off when it gets wet. Congrats—you've made your stick figure dance!

Devotional

Adding the water to the pie plate with the stick figure reminds me of the Bible story where Jesus spoke to the lame man. Turn in your Bible to John 5:1-15 to read all about it.

Jesus has power behind his words, and the lame man had the faith to stand up and take a step. He obeyed the Son of God. What do you think would have happened if the lame man refused to stand and remained lying on the mat?

It's clear that because Jesus had supernatural knowledge, he already knew the lame man's story. Jesus healed the lame man—no questions asked, no requirements on his part. And out of faith, the lame man obeyed Jesus, stood up, and walked. WOW!

God has blessed me at many times in my life, and in more than a few of those instances, I didn't see the blessing until I'd almost missed out on it. Salvation is a free gift—we don't have to do anything to earn it. I think about people I know who have heard the news of what Jesus did on the Cross, yet they aren't taking part in the promise of eternal life. All they have to do is believe like the lame man, and they can receive the greatest and most magnificent gift of all time!

If you haven't chosen to follow Jesus, would you do it now? Don't miss out on another second of the miracle of salvation.

FIZZ TIP: Pray this simple prayer to ask Jesus into your life right now.

"Dear God, I know I'm a sinner, and I ask for your forgiveness. I believe Jesus Christ is Your Son. I believe that He died for my sin and that you raised Him to life. I want to trust Him as my Savior and follow Him as Lord, from this day forward. Guide my life and help me to do your will. I pray this in the name of Jesus. Amen."[1]

Collecting Your Family's Data

Describe what happened when you first added the water.

....

Describe what happened when you moved the water around.

....

What are some of the blessings God has given you?

....

Who in your life needs salvation? How can you pray for them this week?

....

Prayer Time

Magnificent Son, thank you for what you did on the Cross for each of us. May we always have wondrous faith in your unmatched power so we don't doubt you but fearlessly follow where you lead us. Amen.

---

[1] Billy Graham Evangelistic Association, "Start Your New Life with Christ," accessed March 5, 2021, https://lp.billygraham.org/find-peace-with-god/.

PLANTS SEEK LIGHT

Seeking the Light
(John 8:12)

Introduction

When I was in third grade, my school gave me a pine tree. My parents helped me plant the tree, and it began to grow and grow. The next year my sister also got a pine tree, and we planted it next to mine. Fast-forward to today. The pine tree my sister planted is about five feet tall, and the one I planted is twenty feet tall. Why? Well, it has to do with the amount of sunlight the trees receive. In today's experiment, we'll take a look at God's magnificent design of trees and their need for light.

Fizzlebop Supply List

- 2 16-oz (480 mL) mason jars
- Paper towels
- Packet of bean seeds
- Water
- Sunlit windowsill
- Dark cupboard

The Experiment

1. Fill the 2 jars with paper towels by folding the paper towels and pushing them into the jars.

2. Place a bean seed between the paper towels and the side of each jar.

3. Dampen the paper towels, but be careful not to soak them.

4. Place the jars on a sunlit windowsill until you see a sprout (also known as germination).

5. After germination, leave 1 jar on the sill and place 1 jar inside a dark cupboard.

6. Keep the paper towels damp by moistening them every day.

7. Observe the jars and record your findings in the spaces below over the next week.

"Dr. Fizzlebop, what's happening?"

When plants seek light, it's called **phototropism**. But how does it work? Well, plants grow when their cells split, and they need light to do this. The plant cells that are in the shade grow more and more elongated, which causes the stem to bend toward the light.

You may also be curious about how exactly plants use light to grow. Plants have a chemical inside them called **chlorophyll**. This chemical has the ability to convert sunlight into energy and sugar. Chlorophyll is green, which explains why the plant in the cupboard may have been pale or white. Without light, plants can't make chlorophyll, and without chlorophyll, they can't produce energy and sugar, so they will eventually wither and die.

Devotional

Light leads to life! Plants require light to grow. You require light to grow. In John 8:12, Jesus tells us that he is the Light of the World, and by following him, we will have light and life.

Have you ever been afraid of the dark? Maybe you didn't want to go into a dark basement, you got stuck in a closet (That happened to me once!), or you were camping and the woods got dark as night arrived. Not knowing what is around us can be scary or make us anxious.

But when someone turns on the light, our surroundings become visible. We can see there is nothing to be frightened of, and that is reassuring. That's why Jesus promises that if we follow him, we won't be walking in darkness.

Think about the pine tree I planted and the one my sister planted. One grew tall and mighty because it received a lot of light, and one didn't grow because it had only a little light. We are kind of like those trees. When we feed our spirits on the light of Jesus, we grow strong and mighty, and we become courageous and knowledgeable in him. We can feed our spirits by reading the Bible and speaking to God through prayer. One way I take in the light of Jesus is by sitting silently in the middle of the forest and observing God's marvelous creation. He made this wondrous beauty for his people. That fills me with fizztastic joy and awe in his power! It strengthens my faith.

When we don't feed our spirits with God's Word and the light of Christ, they remain weak. Like trees, our spirits need light to grow to wondrous heights and join the wonder and beauty of God's magnificent creation.

So let me ask you, will you follow Jesus? Will you say yes and trust him all of your days?

Collecting Your Family's Data

Begin recording observations after the jars have been separated—one in the cupboard and one on the windowsill.

Day 1 Observations:
Seed in the light:

Seed in the dark:

Day 3 Observations:
Seed in the light:

Seed in the dark:

Day 6 Observations:
Seed in the light:

Seed in the dark:

....

After a week, describe the differences between the seed growing in the light and the one growing in the dark.

....

How can you start feeding your spirit with Jesus' light?

....

Prayer Time

Jesus, you are the Light, and we want to follow you. Help us to be courageous even in times of darkness, knowing that if we turn to you, we'll be able to find our way. Amen.

GROWING MOLD

Jesus Raises Lazarus
(John 11:1-44)

Introduction

It's alive! Or it will be once it starts to grow. Either way, I've always wanted to say that, as any true scientist does. Today at Fizzlebop Labs, we're going to begin growing something you're typically told to avoid: mold. You might be shocked by the stupendous amount of mold that grows on the bread in this experiment—but if you're anything like me, it'll make you start washing your hands a lot more!

WARNING! This experiment involves mold. Safety first! Do not eat the moldy bread.

Fizzlebop Supply List

- 3 16-oz (480 mL) mason jars with lids
- Permanent marker
- 3 pieces of white bread
  FIZZ TIP: Bread fresh from the bakery works best in this experiment, as it contains fewer preservatives (which often keep mold from growing).
- Tongs
- 1 tsp (5 mL) water
- Dark place (pantry or coat closet)
- Magnifying glass

The Experiment

1. Line up the jars. Label the jars A, B, and C.

   FIZZ TIP: You can write directly on glass jars with a permanent marker and easily wash it off when you're done.

2. Pick up the first piece of bread with tongs, place the bread in Jar A, and screw on the lid. Don't touch it with your hands!

3. Sprinkle a tiny bit of water on another piece of bread, and leave it outside your home for 20 minutes. Place it in Jar B and screw on the lid.

4. Sprinkle the third piece of bread with water, then rub it between your hands and along the kitchen counter. Place this piece of bread in Jar C and screw on the lid.

5 Place the jars in a dark place, like your pantry or coat closet, and check on them every 3 days for 9 days. Be sure to record and observe what you see at each 3-day interval, using the magnifying glass.

"Dr. Fizzlebop, what's happening?"

Mold spores and bacteria are everywhere—you just can't see them with your eyes. Though a surface may look clean, contaminants could still be thriving. If food comes into contact with a surface that hasn't been cleaned—or with hands that haven't been washed—it's likely that mold and bacteria will be transferred to the food and will start to grow. Wash your hands with soap and warm water to get rid of it!

Devotional

Sometimes, really bad things happen that feel confusing and hard to understand. Jesus' good friends Martha and Mary knew all about that. When their brother, Lazarus, got very sick, they sent a messenger to ask Jesus to come pray for Lazarus. They knew Jesus healed people, and as some of his closest friends, they knew Jesus would heal Lazarus.

But he didn't. And Lazarus died.

Why in the world would Jesus not heal Lazarus, of all people? Lazarus not only died but remained in the grave a whole four days before Jesus finally came to town. Lazarus's body was not in good shape—kind of like your slice of bread after sitting in a dark place for a few days.

When Martha heard Jesus was coming, she went out to meet him. "Why were you not here?" she wanted to know. "If you had been here, my brother would be alive!"

Have you ever wanted to ask Jesus something like that?

Here's the good news! Martha, who knew him well on earth, knew it was okay to ask him anything. And she did!

Even though Martha didn't understand why Jesus hadn't come sooner, she must've impressed him with her next words. "But even now I know that God will give you whatever you ask."

When Mary rushed out to meet Jesus, she fell at his feet and wept. And you know what Jesus did? Jesus—the Son of God, who knew what he was about to do to make things better—wept with Mary! He saw her tears and was moved with compassion for her pain and grief, and he wept with her. (I think this is the most beautiful and precious glimpse into Jesus' heart that I have seen in the Bible. Isn't it fizztastic?)

I don't want to ruin the surprise by telling you what happened, but just know that weeping together wasn't the end of the story. Not at all! Check out John 11:1-44 to read the whole thing and find out the amazing ending.

Now, whether or not Jesus does a miracle like this in your confusing situation, let me give you some more good news. When we're with Jesus for eternity, he will wipe every tear from our eyes. With him, there will be no more death or sorrow or mourning or crying or pain! Now *that's* something to leap about!

FIZZ FACT: John 11:35 (NIV), "Jesus wept," is the shortest verse in the Bible. Take a moment and memorize it. Then remember that it may be short, but it's also very powerful.

Collecting Your Family's Data

Record the progress of each piece of bread below.

Day 3 Observations:
Jar A:

Jar B:

....

Jar C:

....

Day 6 Observations:
Jar A:

....

Jar B:

....

Jar C:

....

Day 9 Observations:
Jar A:

....

Jar B:

....

Jar C:

....

Which piece of bread grew mold first?

....

Describe any differences in the mold (size, color, texture) you observed on day 9.

....

What was something difficult that happened in your life that you didn't understand?

....

When you don't have answers to life's confusing questions, how does it make you feel that Jesus weeps with you? Why?

....

Prayer Time

Jesus, you wept with Mary and Martha. We know that you also weep with us in our sorrows, provide comfort and peace, and carry us when we can no longer walk. Thank you for always being here with your arms wide and ready to hold us. Amen.

FIZZ EXTRA: Mummy Hop

Wrap someone in your family in toilet paper (with their permission, of course!), and see if they can hop around without falling down. Wrap a few more people up and try racing each other!

Send a video of the fun, and we may post it on the Fizzlebop Labs website.

Find the MUMMY HOP project at Fizzlebop.com, or scan this QR Code and click FIZZ EXTRA to upload videos and see other fun clips.

FOAM OVERFLOW

Joy Overflowing
(John 15:9-11)

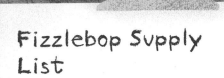

Introduction

I'm ecstatic about this experiment. Why? Because foam is my second-favorite substance (inferior only to fizz, of course!). And today is all about foam—lots of foam. When this foam erupts from your plastic bottle, you're going to be fizztastically impressed. The neato thing about this experiment is that you can scale it up (which means make it as big as you want). I suggest following the instructions below to start and then discussing as a family if you want to go bigger. But have fun with this overflowing foam!

Fizzlebop Supply List

- Safety goggles
- Rubber gloves
- Funnel
- 2 L (68 oz) plastic bottle
- 1/2 cup (120 mL) 20-volume hydrogen peroxide

  FIZZ TIP: 20-volume is a 6% solution that is stronger than what most pharmacies carry. You can usually find it in a beauty supply store. The 3% hydrogen peroxide sold at pharmacies will cause a smaller reaction, but it will make the foam safe to touch.

- Food coloring
- Liquid dish soap
- 1 tbsp (10 g) dry yeast
- 3 tbsp (45 mL) warm water
- 1-cup measuring cup
- Spoon

219

The Experiment

1. Put on your safety goggles and rubber gloves.

2. Use the funnel to carefully pour ½ cup (120 mL) of hydrogen peroxide into the plastic bottle.

3. Add 10 drops of your favorite color of food coloring to the bottle.

4. Add 1 tbsp (15 mL) of liquid dish soap to the bottle.

5. Put the cap on the bottle and swish it around to mix the contents.

WARNING! This experiment requires hydrogen peroxide. Safety first! We also recommend reading the caution labels on each container. It can be messy, so be sure to protect the area you are working in. You may be wondering, *Is the foam safe to touch?* The reaction usually breaks the hydrogen peroxide down, leaving mostly soapy water and yeast. However, some unreacted hydrogen peroxide can remain, which may irritate the skin and eyes. For that reason, we recommend you do not touch the foam.

6 Combine the warm water and the yeast in the measuring cup. Mix for about 30 seconds.

FIZZ TIP: This mixture should have the consistency of melted ice cream. If not, stir in a bit more water.

7 Use the funnel to pour the water-yeast mix into the bottle. Step back and observe.

8 Be sure to clean up when you're done with your observations. Since the foam produced is just water, soap, and oxygen, you can clean the foam up with a sponge. Any leftover liquid can be safely dumped down the drain.

"Dr. Fizzlebop, what's happening?"

This amazing overflow of foam is known as elephant toothpaste. In our experiment, the yeast acted as a catalyst (which means it sped up the reaction). The yeast broke apart the oxygen from the hydrogen peroxide super fast. And because of the speed, the reaction created lots and lots of bubbles, all of which contain oxygen. You may not have noticed, but the plastic bottle warmed up as the reaction occurred. That's because this was an exothermic reaction—which means it released energy, creating heat.

One more thing: this experiment may be called elephant toothpaste, but you should never put it in or near your mouth.

Devotional

Have you ever been so excited that you jumped up and down? What were you thrilled about? Maybe a surprise visit from your grandparents? An amazing gift you really wanted? Super fizztastic news?

I remember when I was a kid on the happiest of all mornings—Christmas! But when I got tired of playing with my new things, my happiness would fizzle (not the good fizzle, either). Know what I'm talking about?

How would you like to have the kind of joy that never fizzles out but fills you up and refills you when you're drained? I've discovered the secret to finding that joyous treasure, and it overflows even more awesomely than the foam overflowed in our experiment!

Jesus had been the disciples' rabbi (which also means teacher) for three years, and they depended on him. He knew they'd be upset and afraid when he got arrested, and they'd deeply grieve when his enemies killed him. So he warned them of what would happen—but also gave them hope.

I challenge you to read John 14 through 17 to get the whole story and read all of Jesus' final words for yourself.

Jesus said he doesn't call his followers servants, but friends. How fizztastic is that, to be a friend of God? Can you imagine how cool it'd be to be a disciple and watch him heal people and perform miracles?

"I have loved you even as the Father has loved me," Jesus told his disciples. "Remain in my love. When you obey my commandments, you remain in my love, just as I obey my Father's commandments and remain in his love. I have told you these things so that you will be filled with my joy. Yes, your joy will overflow!" (John 15:9-11).

I pretty much know whether I'm obeying God's command-ments or not. And if I'm not sure, I can always turn to the Bible. If I ignore his commandments and say something mean to my brother, I feel God's sadness. (He wants his kids to love each other!) If I do something I know is wrong, it hurts me—and it hurts God. So, you see, the rules are important because our relationships with God and each other are important.

How would you like to have complete joy that can't be taken away? Have you discovered how to find it?

FIZZ FACT: When you remain in Jesus' love, your joy will overflow just like a big bottle of elephant toothpaste!

Collecting Your Family's Data

Describe what the reaction looked like.

....

What do you think would change if you added the dry yeast without mixing it with water?

....

When have you felt overflowing joy? What caused it, and how long did it last?

....

What is the connection between joy and God's rules?

....

What can you do to pursue overflowing joy?

....

Prayer Time

Magnificent Son, please fill us with your overflowing joy. We want to follow your rules and grow in our relationship with you so that we may experience your complete and real joy! Amen.

MAKING WAVES

Paul Shipwrecked
(Acts 27:27-44)

Introduction

Have you ever stood on a beach, right where the waves roll in and out? The waves pass over your feet and onto the shore, and then as the water pulls back, it takes sand with it and you feel your feet sink deeper. The waves never stop coming, one after the other. Some might actually look like they are rolling, while others might swell and crash. Can you hear them in your imagination? While the motion of waves up and down is mesmerizing when you simply observe them, it can make others feel seasick if they're riding on them in a boat. In today's experiment, we're going to take a look at the rolling motion of waves.

Fizzlebop Supply List

- Clean 20-oz (600 mL) plastic bottle (label removed) with cap
- 3/4 cup (180 mL) water
- Blue food coloring
- 1 cup (240 mL) clear vegetable oil

The Experiment

1. Pour the water into the bottle.

2. Add 3 drops of food coloring.

3. Pour the vegetable oil into the bottle.

4. Screw the cap on tightly.

5. Roll the bottle on its side and let the water and oil separate and settle for 3 minutes.

   FIZZ FACT: The water will sink to the bottom and the oil will rise to the top because water is denser than oil.

6. Grab both ends of the bottle and tip it back and forth. Make some waves and observe.

7. Move the bottle back and forth a bit harder (but not so much that you mix the oil and water).

"Dr. Fizzlebop, what's happening?"

As you move the bottle, you simulate wind, which creates the rolling motion of the waves. A wave is a complex blend of energy and water. If you have ever watched waves crash against the seashore—or become seasick on a boat—you know without a doubt that waves move. What you may not realize is that the water in the waves moves very little—it's actually energy transferring across the water. Think about a bedsheet. If you take hold of two corners on the same side and give it a flick or a swish, the sheet moves like a wave, but the fabric itself doesn't move away from you. Only the energy you flick across the sheet moves to the other end.

FIZZ FACT: The highest part of a wave is called the crest, while the lowest part is called the trough.

Devotional

The apostle Paul is well known as a follower of Jesus—in fact, he wrote several books of the Bible! But Paul didn't always know Jesus. He experienced one of the most miraculous conversions in history (which you can read about in Acts 9:1-19). He changed from a man who persecuted (which means disliked and harmed) Christians to someone who trusted Jesus and told many other people about him.

Once Paul came face-to-face with Jesus, he could not deny the truth that the Messiah had come. So he began a ministry to preach to all the known world, to travel, to write letters to the local churches, and to encourage those who believed. Paul began making waves throughout the world, which is another way to say he was disrupting what was normal.

Like Jesus, Paul was despised by many of the religious leaders of the time. They wanted Paul arrested and thrown in prison, simply for sharing his belief that Jesus is the Son of God.

Open your Bible and read Acts 27:27-44.

Paul was a prisoner on a ship out at sea, and the soldiers around him wanted him dead. As a dangerous storm that lasted weeks threatened to sink the boat and drown everyone on board, Paul continued to stand steadfast in his faith.

Paul boldly proclaimed his belief in God when he told the soldiers and sailors that he had received a visit from an angel. What I find interesting is that though these people did not like him, they believed his words. Paul continued to show his love and compassion for them by offering wisdom from God on how to survive in their perilous (which means dangerous) situation. Paul's courage was strong in the midst of the storm and his tough situation as a prisoner.

God saw them through, and because Paul faithfully delivered God's messages to the soldiers and sailors, they all survived.

I hope that I will always have the courage to boldly proclaim what God has done and is doing. That kind of boldness makes waves that will ripple throughout the world and change lives.

Collecting Your Family's Data

Describe the size and shape of the waves in your bottle.

....

What happened when you moved the bottle with more force?

....

Do you find it hard or easy to proclaim your faith? Can you think of a time when you were able to share about Jesus with someone else?

....

Prayer Time

Amazing Creator, please give us opportunities to spread the wonderful news about your Son and your plan for forgiveness. Help us to make good waves that reach the farthest corners of the world. Amen.

FIZZ INFLATOR

God Fills Your Heart with Love

(Romans 5:3-5)

Introduction

Greetings! You already know how much I love fizz, and today we get to use a lot—and I mean a *lot*—of fizz. I feel fizztastic just thinking about it, and you should too! So gather all the scientists in your house and get ready for another fun-filled fizzy experiment.

Fizzlebop Supply List

- Small balloon
- 1/2 cup (120 mL) vinegar
- Small plastic bottle (20 oz or 600 mL)
- Funnel
- Baking soda
- String (about 2 feet or 0.6 meters long)
- Ruler

The Experiment

1. Loosen up the balloon by stretching it a few times. You can do this by blowing it up, then letting all the air out (and repeating that a few times).

2. Carefully pour the vinegar into the bottle.

3. Fit the opening of the balloon around the small end of the funnel and fill it more than halfway full with baking soda.

4. This next part could get tricky, so work together. Carefully put the balloon's neck over the neck of the bottle without letting any baking soda into the bottle.

5. Lift the balloon, allowing the baking soda to sprinkle from the balloon into the bottle.

6 Observe what happens as the vinegar and baking soda mix. Wrap the string around the balloon once. Then measure the string on a ruler to find the diameter.

7 Try this again using a different amount of baking soda. Measure the diameter and observe whether it changed.

"Dr. Fizzlebop, what's happening?"

Did you know that baking soda is considered a **base** and vinegar is an acid? When baking soda and vinegar mix, they cause a chemical reaction—the reaction between the base and the acid creates carbon dioxide gas. And because gas expands, it fills the bottle, but the bottle's sides don't grow with the gas. The excess gas goes up into the balloon, causing it to inflate.

Devotional

As a young scientist, I often wondered what would happen if I attached enough balloons to a chair. Would they lift me into the air? What if I filled the balloons with something besides helium? Well, I believe in research before starting an experiment, and I also believe in safety first. I never did attempt my idea because I discovered I had a major problem: I'm afraid of heights!

But in my research, I realized that you couldn't fill a balloon with just anything—in fact, some gases used to fill balloons can be dangerous. It is believed that a famous airship named the *Hindenburg* caught fire many years ago because of static electricity and a leak of hydrogen gas. The fire spread and destroyed the airship. And if you fill a balloon with water, it won't float up into the air, though you could sure have a lot of family fun with water balloons. Hydrogen can cause fire, and water is too heavy, so you've got to fill your balloon with the right thing to make it work.

Our hearts are the same way. I'm not talking about the

muscle in your body that pumps blood, but the heart that allows us to feel and show love. What we put into our hearts matters. If we are around people who use foul language, we may find ourselves eventually using those words ourselves. Or if we spend time with friends who gossip and lie, we may find ourselves doing the same without really thinking about it. If we eat unhealthy foods, our body may become run-down and more likely to get sick. What we consume affects our body, mind, and heart. These things can even change how we view the world and can slowly move us away from God's plan for our life.

But there's another way! Read Romans 5:3-5 to see what God wants to do in our hearts.

We can trust that God loves us, and he gives the Holy Spirit to guide us each day and fill our hearts with hope and love. As the challenges of life help us develop strong character traits grounded in our hope of salvation, we'll draw closer to God. His love will fill our hearts—kind of like the balloon in our experiment—and even spill over to others!

Collecting Your Family's Data

How quickly did the chemical reaction start once the base and acid were combined?

....

Did the balloon expand to different sizes when you used different amounts of baking soda? If yes, write down your measurement of the balloon's size every time you used a different amount of baking soda.

....

We know that God loves us—we can read about how much in John 3:16. List people in your life who love you, and thank God for them!

....

Prayer Time

In your prayer time, share something that isn't good for your heart and mind. Ask God to help you avoid and remove this from your life. Praise him for filling your heart with his love.

BLACK LIGHT BEVERAGE

Consume the Good Stuff

(Romans 12:1-2)

Introduction

Has anyone ever told you, "What goes in must come out"? This principle applies to many things in life: what we eat, what we see, what we hear, and more. Have you ever been watching a television show with content that was a bit violent or scary? Or listened to music with unsavory lyrics? Did any images from the show stick with you or give you a bad dream? Did the vulgar word you heard come to mind or even across your lips when you were frustrated or angry? We don't immediately see the effects of what we listen to or watch. But those negative (which means bad) influences can sometimes find their way into our minds or our words. Not only are we then spreading the negative content, but we're making our Amazing Creator sad. Think about this while you're conducting today's experiment and reading the devotional.

Fizzlebop Supply List

- 16-oz (480 mL) mason jar
- 1 cup (240 mL) tonic water
- 1/2 cup (120 mL) lemon-lime soda
- Ice cubes
- Black light

  FIZZ TIP: A black light flashlight is ideal.

- Red food coloring

233

The Experiment

1. Pour 1 cup (240 mL) tonic water and ½ cup (120 mL) lemon-lime soda into the jar. Add four ice cubes.

2. Take a drink from the jar.

3. Turn off the lights and turn on the black light. Shine the black light at the jar. Observe and record what you see.

4. Turn the lights on and add 3 drops of red food coloring to the jar.

5. Turn off the lights again and turn on the black light. Observe and record what you see.

6. Drink or discard the liquid.

FIZZ TIP: If you're not a fan of tonic water, you can make ice cubes from the tonic water. Just put the cubes in the soda. You'll see the same effect when you turn on the black light.

"Dr. Fizzlebop, what's happening?"

Tonic water contains small amounts of a substance called quinine. Quinine has a special property: when it interacts with a black light, it appears blue. It's really that super-simple. Look around your house and see what other objects glow under your black light.

Devotional

Reflect on today's experiment. If you followed the instructions, you drank some of the tonic water before you shone the black light on it. Think of the tonic water as the media (music or television) you take in—or the conversations you usually have with friends. Maybe you've watched a show that was just over the line of being wholesome (which means pure), and a character hurt someone else in a graphic way. Maybe a lyric in a song you heard was inappropriate or vulgar, and your mind took it in and catalogued it before you even realized what had happened. Or maybe you hung out with friends who use inappropriate language, and you found yourself saying some words you knew you shouldn't say.

If the tonic water is like the media you take in or the conversations you have, the quinine (the stuff that glows) is like the unsavory content. You can't see the glowing quinine once you've drunk it, just like you can't always see the effects of media or conversations. But it's there. I don't mean to be all doom and gloom, but I want you to think about the consequences (which means effects) that the media and your friends can have on you. The choices you make when watching television, playing video games, or listening to music—or even the people you choose to spend time with—can have consequences on your heart, mind, and soul.

Read Romans 12:1-2. If we fill our minds and hearts with the things of the world—especially the negative ones— we aren't leaving room for the wondrous, magnificent, stupendous ways and ideas of our Amazing Creator. As a family, you can unite to make your home a place for choices that will please and delight God. From your grandparents down to your youngest sibling, you can join in protecting each other's hearts, minds, and souls.

Collecting Your Family's Data

Describe the appearance of your drink mixture when you turned on the black light.

....

Describe any changes you observed when you added the red food coloring.

....

What do you think would happen if you added other colors of food coloring to the liquid? Give it a try!

....

Have you ever been watching a show or listening to music when you realized it might not be the best choice? What did you do?

....

What are some ways your family can encourage each other to be mindful about media choices?

....

Prayer Time

Take some time as a family to discuss the shows and music you listen to. Maybe even make a list of the ones that you're not sure about. Then spend some time praying as a family for discernment over those choices and for protection from temptation. This is also a good time to seek forgiveness if you've been making unwise media choices.

BEND a BONE with VINEGAR

Foundation in Jesus
(1 Corinthians 3:11)

Introduction

Have you ever heard that you should drink milk to make your bones stronger? Well, it's actually the calcium contained in the milk that strengthens your bones. Indeed, there are many other foods and drinks that can provide calcium for your bones. In fact, today we're going to experiment with what happens when we remove that calcium from a bone. Now, don't worry—we're not doing any surgery, just a nifty science experiment.

Fizzlebop Supply List

- Chicken bone (no meat or skin)
- 16-oz (480 mL) mason jar with lid
- Vinegar (enough to cover the bone in the jar)

The Experiment

1. First enjoy a family dinner featuring chicken, then save at least 1 leg bone.

2. Rinse the bone to remove any remaining meat or skin.

3. Observe the bone and record your observations. Notice how hard it is. Gently try bending it.

4. Place the chicken bone into the jar, then pour the vinegar into the jar. Cover the jar with a lid.

5. Let the bone and vinegar sit for 1 day. Then remove the bone from the jar, but do not discard the vinegar. Rinse off the bone and compare it to your previous observations.

Place the bone back in the jar of vinegar. After 2 more days, remove the bone.

Rinse off the bone and compare it to your previous observations.

"Dr. Fizzlebop, what's happening?"

Vinegar is a mild acid, and therefore it is strong enough to dissolve the calcium in the chicken bone. Once this calcium is gone, there is nothing to keep the bone firm. All that remains is the soft, bendy tissue of the bone. That's why, although your bone looks similar to how it did before, it can now bend. Intriguing, isn't it?

Devotional

Bones are the foundation of our bodies, and if all the calcium is gone, they become like rubber. Our bodies need calcium to be strong and have structure. Have you ever seen one of those tall inflatable tube dancers—you know, the ones made of colorful fabric that look like people? Their arms wave this way and that, and their tubelike bodies curve, twist, and bend in odd, rubbery ways. Without bones, our bodies would be like this.

Strong foundations are vital to many things in our lives. What if every time you sat in a chair, the legs bent under you? Or what if the foundation of your house was like a bunch of Jell-O blocks? The whole house would collapse! What about your faith? What if it wasn't built on the firm foundation of Jesus? In 1 Corinthians, Paul tells the church of Corinth how important it is that the foundation of their faith is Jesus, not the different teachers they've had.

First Corinthians 3:11 says, "No one can lay any foundation other than the one we already have—Jesus Christ."

At times, your faith will be tested. If it's resting on

someone or something that can fail, your faith will be like the house built on Jell-O.

What a wonderful thing that we can build our faith on the firm foundation of Jesus—who will never fail us—and that we don't have to be like the flimsy tube dancer flailing its body around in the wind. In the same way that our bones need calcium, our faith needs daily doses of Jesus. Give your spirit what it needs: read your Bible every day, and talk to God through prayer.

Now take a minute to see who in your family can make the funniest impression of one of those tube dancers!

Collecting Your Family's Data

Time	Observations
Before being placed in vinegar	
1 day in vinegar	
3 days in vinegar	

Based on your observations, does the length of time the bone is in vinegar affect how much it bends? Why do you think that is?

Be honest and evaluate your faith foundation below. Do you put your trust in Jesus or in other people or things?

What can you do each day to help your faith grow strong?

240

Prayer Time

As a family, pray for each other by name—that each of you would lay a solid foundation in your relationship with Jesus, so that when times are challenging, you'll be able to stand strong.

CLEAN PENNIES with VINEGAR

Cleansing from Sin
(1 Corinthians 6:11)

Introduction

Have you ever heard of an **atom**? Not Adam, as in the first man, but *atom*, as in a very tiny particle. In today's experiment, we're going to learn a bit about how atoms combine into molecules, how molecules can break apart, and even how atoms work at a much smaller level involving **protons**, **electrons**, and **neutrons**. This may all sound complex, but when you see the science in action, it'll become clean—I mean, clear. Though our pennies *will* get clean, and you may even notice a little of my favorite thing—that's right, fizz!

Fizzlebop Supply List

- 1/4 cup (60 mL) white vinegar
- 1 tsp (5 g) salt
- Glass mixing bowl
- Spoon
- Timer (watch or phone)
- 20 old pennies

  FIZZ TIP: Use pennies that are no longer shiny.

- Water
- 2 clean steel nails
- Tape
- Clean steel screw

The Experiment

Pour the vinegar and salt into the bowl. Stir the mixture until the salt dissolves.

Set the timer for 10 seconds, and dip one penny halfway into the liquid while the timer counts down. Observe what you see and record it in the chart.

Reset the timer for 10 seconds, and put all 20 pennies into the bowl. Start the timer and observe what changes.

Leave the pennies in the mixture for 5 more minutes, then take them out and rinse them with water. Observe and record the results.

Fully submerge one nail and the screw in the liquid. Lean the second nail against the inside of the bowl, so that only half of the nail is in the liquid. Secure the top of the nail to the side of the bowl with a small piece of tape to keep it from slipping.

After 10 minutes, take a look at the nails and screw. Observe and record. Any fizz?

7 Put all the objects—pennies, nails, and screw—back in the mixture. Let them sit for 1 hour, then observe and record a final time.

"Dr. Fizzlebop, what's happening?"

Pennies contain copper, and copper is made up of **minuscule** (which means tiny) particles called atoms. The copper atoms on the surface of the penny naturally combine with the oxygen in the air and form a compound called copper oxide, which makes the pennies look dirty. Copper oxide can easily be broken down with a weak acid and salt mixture, which is what we made by combining the salt with vinegar. Blue copper ions (positively charged) are produced and are dissolved in the solution, making the pennies shiny again.

When the pennies underwent their chemical reaction in the vinegar-salt acid, some of their copper atoms came loose and began floating freely as copper ions in our mixture. Then we added two steel nails and the screw to the acid mixture, which began dissolving some of the iron from the nails and screw.

Before we began the experiment, the nails and screw were neutral (no charge), but because our reaction released iron ions, the nails and screw lost protons (positively charged particles), switching their charge from neutral to negative. Opposites attract, so the negatively charged nails and screw attracted the positive copper ions floating in the solution. Before you knew it, you had copper-coated nails and a screw.

You probably didn't realize all the reactions between atoms, molecules, and ions taking place in this seemingly simple experiment, but now you know. And to think, God designed each intricate detail: protons, neutrons, electrons, and all.

Devotional

Shiny, clean pennies are swell! It's neato to see such a dramatic transformation from old and dirty to shiny and new. I'm not saying I'm a germophobe, but I have a zealous preference for clean things. I even give my coins a hand-sanitizer bath when I get change at a store.

If you have a few more dirty pennies lying around, look at them closely. Now compare them to the clean pennies. What details can you and your family spot on the clean pennies that maybe you can't see on the dirty ones? You may notice that the penny itself reflects light way better than it did when it was dirty. Oooh, shiny.

I've been performing this vinegar experiment ever since I was a kid. It's absolutely marvelous. Whenever I got coins for doing my chores or extra work around the house, I would take those coins and give them a good vinegar soaking. I had the shiniest pocket of coins in my entire town. On a sunny day, I would take out one of my coins and observe how its cleanness allowed the sun to reflect off it in a spectacular display.

In the same way, we are called to reflect the light of God to those around us. But this is impossible unless we are cleaned by the sacrifice Jesus made. Read 1 Corinthians 6:11 to see how Jesus completely cleans us of all our sin.

I've got an idea for you. Why not keep one of those shiny pennies in your pocket wherever you go? Here's why. Whenever you reach in your pocket and feel the penny, you'll be reminded to be a light for Jesus.

Collecting Your Family's Data

Time & Object	Observations
1 penny half-submerged after 10 seconds	
20 pennies after 10 seconds	

Time & Object	Observations
20 pennies after 5 minutes	
2 nails and a screw after 10 minutes	
2 nails and a screw after 1 hour	
20 pennies after 1 hour	

Describe the way the pennies changed during the experiment.

Do you think other acids (lemon juice or orange juice) would work as well? Test it out!

Does the mixture work on other dirty coins (nickels, dimes)? Why or why not?

How can you be a reflection of God's light today?

Prayer Time

Amazing Creator, we are thankful that you cleanse us from our sins. We ask for your help so we can shine brightly for you. Amen.

TASTE TESTING
without SMELL

We Are a Pleasing Aroma
(2 Corinthians 2:14-16)

Introduction

Broccoli is a favorite vegetable of mine—maybe you like it too! But there is probably someone in your family who doesn't like it at all. It's just that some foods taste better than others to different people. I play a jelly bean game with my little Fizzlebops where I give them some jelly beans that taste good and some that do not. The worst thing is, all the beans look the same, so they don't know what they're about to taste until they chew the little bean! So what gives us the ability to experience all these unique flavors? This super-simple experiment shows that there's a lot more to taste than you might think.

WARNING! This experiment requires a vegetable peeler and a knife. Safety first!

Fizzlebop Supply List

- Vegetable peeler
- Potato
- Apple
- Knife
- Family members

The Experiment

1   Peel the potato and the apple (or ask an adult to do it for you).

2   Cut a 1-inch (2.5 cm) cube per person from the potato and the apple.

    FIZZ TIP: Make each piece the same shape and size so you can't tell the difference between them.

3   Set a piece of apple and a piece of potato in front of each person.

4   Close your eyes and mix up the two pieces.

5   Hold your nose and eat each piece, one at a time.

6   Observe and record what you taste or don't taste. Ask your family members for their findings too.

"Dr. Fizzlebop, what's happening?"

Your mouth and nose are connected by the same airway, which allows your body to taste and smell foods at the same time. Holding your nose while tasting the two cubes makes it difficult to tell the difference between them. This is because your sense of taste can recognize salty, sweet, bitter, and sour—but when they are combined with your sense of smell, many other individual tastes or flavors become recognizable. The brain relies on multiple senses to interpret the world, so by limiting your senses, you make it more difficult for your brain to gather the information it needs.

Devotional

God created everyone, and he gave us our senses, too, like the fizztastic sense of smell. Well, it's fizztastic as long as there is good-smelling stuff around, like Mom's fresh bread as it comes out of the oven. Warm bread with butter melting on it . . . *mmmmm*! Now I'm hungry!

Of course, this sense isn't so great around icky-smelling things, like rotten fish or stink bugs. And I don't know about you, but I definitely have to hold my nose around soiled (which means dirty) diapers!

What are some of your favorite aromas? I love the clean scent of rain or freshly popped popcorn. Oh, and the aroma of turtle brownies as they bake! I sniff the air, anticipating how good they're gonna taste!

What do you think some of God's favorite smells are? Least favorite? Open your Bible to 2 Corinthians 2:14-16 and let's have a look!

When we allow God to make us his "captives" (which means we're bound to him by love and devotion), we're led along in Christ's victorious procession. And as we marvelously march along in life, God uses us to share with others the knowledge of Christ that's like a sweet perfume! Then the aromas of love, joy, peace, kindness, patience, and hope not only please the senses of those whom God seeks, but those fragrances are tremendously pleasing to God himself!

Of course, there will always be people who don't like this scent, as we see in verses 15 and 16. But the most important thing is what God thinks, and he loves this aroma even more than my grandma's homemade apple pie!

Have you put on your life-giving perfume today? Remember: it's not a scent that you can concoct or create on your own in the lab. The fragrance of the knowledge of God comes from a close relationship with him and time spent studying his life letter to us (the Bible). That's how we learn all we need to walk in grace, serve with kindness, and show the magnificent love of God to all we meet.

Collecting Your Family's Data

Was anyone unable to taste the difference between the apple and potato?

....

What other foods might you be able to test this with? How about a carrot and a sweet potato?

....

How can you spritz yourself with the fragrance of the knowledge of Christ every day?

....

Imagine how much God could use your "sweet-smelling" family to draw others to himself! Who would you like your family to show love and kindness to this week?

....

Prayer Time

Amazing Creator, thank you for making our senses and allowing us to experience this wondrous world you made. We hope that we can be a pleasing aroma to you and to others by being marvelous examples of your love. Amen.

FIZZ EXTRA: Cilantro versus Anise

So I have a theory: If you like cilantro, you won't like anise, and vice versa. Test my theory with this super-simple—and perhaps tasty—FIZZ EXTRA, and survey your friends and family on their preference of cilantro, anise, or both.

Find the CILANTRO VERSUS ANISE survey at Fizzlebop.com, or scan this QR code and click or tap FIZZ EXTRA.

FIZZY ORANGE

Fruits of the Spirit

(Galatians 5:22-23)

Introduction

Indeed, fizz is one of my favorite things and so is fruit! This experiment's super simplicity means it will be done before you know it, but it'll leave a lasting taste for more fun fizzy science. Fruit is the theme for the day at Fizzlebop Labs as we learn about the fruits of the Spirit and how we can grow them in our lives each and every day. But first, fizz!

BAKING SODA

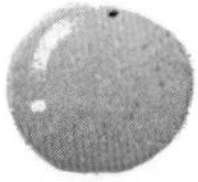

Fizzlebop Supply List

- Orange or clementine
- 1/2 tsp (2 g) baking soda

The Experiment

1. Peel the orange or clementine and separate into slices.

2. Dip a slice into the baking soda.

3. Take a bite and observe what happens in your mouth.

"Dr. Fizzlebop, what's happening?"

Oranges and other citrus fruits are filled with citric acid. This is a safe acid, and it's what gives oranges, lemons, and limes their sourness. Baking soda is a base—the opposite of an acid. Baking soda is also safe, but it doesn't taste very good on its own, and if you eat too much of it, you'll get a stomachache. When acids and bases mix, the result is chemistry in action. As the citric acid and baking soda combine, the reaction makes gazillions of carbon dioxide bubbles. Carbon dioxide is the same gas you breathe out, and the same one that makes soda fizztastically fizzy!

Devotional

First, a challenge. Can anyone in your family say all nine fruits of the Spirit without looking in the Bible? If not, how many can you write down as a family? Give it a shot in the spaces below.

....

....

....

....

....

....

....

....

Now take a look at Galatians 5:22-23 to see if you got them right. How'd you do?

While the experiment today involved a real piece of fruit,

the Bible isn't talking about the kind of fruit you can eat. And growing the fruits of the Spirit isn't super-simple the way this experiment was.

While I strive to have love, joy, peace, patience, kindness, goodness, faithfulness, gentleness, and self-control, I'm not always successful. Sometimes I'm not kind, or I don't feel joyful. Sometimes I lack faith or self-control. It doesn't mean God loves me less, but it does mean I need to check my heart and my focus. Have I been reading my Bible, praying, and communicating with God regularly? Have I been seeking Jesus and listening to the Holy Spirit?

We're human, and we're far from perfect, and that's why the verse says, "the Holy Spirit produces this kind of fruit in our lives." It's not us alone doing the work. God gave us the Holy Spirit to be with us daily and to communicate with us. None of this goodness is because of us, but because of what God does through us and in our lives.

When you review the fruits of the Spirit, you can see that there is nothing bad in them. They are all good for you, and they are all good for your family and friends. By living them out as best you can, you're sure to see great things in your life as the fruits of the Spirit produce other sorts of fruit such as friendship, hope, opportunity, and more.

Collecting Your Family's Data

Describe the sensation of the reaction in your mouth.

Do you think the reaction would have been the same with a lemon or lime? If you have those fruits around, test it out!

Which fruits of the Spirit are the easiest for you to live out each day? Which ones are harder?

What can you do to grow more of the fruits of the Spirit in your life?

....

Prayer Time

Amazing Creator, thank you for giving us the Holy Spirit to be with us each day. We pray that we'll listen as the Spirit speaks and guides us. May we do our best to live out the fruits of the Spirit. Amen.

WATER PURIFICATION

Purification

(1 John 1:9)

Introduction

Greetings, scientists! Today we'll be working with water. Did you know that your body is something like 60% water? That's more than half—wow! You, as a human, need water to live, and there is a whole lot of water on Earth: 71% of the Earth's surface is covered with water. Sadly, though, it is estimated that 1 out of 3 people do not have access to safe drinking water. You may be asking the same question I did: How do we make water safe to drink? In today's experiment, we're going to make a water purifier. Ready?

WARNING! This experiment requires scissors. Safety first!

Fizzlebop Supply List

- 3 cups (900 g) dirt
- 2 cups (480 mL) water
- Mixing bowl
- Scissors
- 2 L (68 oz) plastic soda bottle with cap
- 2 cotton balls
- 1 cup (50 g) activated charcoal

  FIZZ TIP: Activated charcoal is often available at pet stores.

- Gallon plastic bag
- Rubber mallet
- 1 cup (350 g) sand
- 1 cup (400 g) gravel
- 32-oz (960 mL) mason jar

The Experiment

1. Make some muddy water by combining the dirt and water in the mixing bowl.

2. Use scissors to cut off the bottom of the plastic soda bottle. (Keep the cap on.)

3. Set the bottle on top of the mason jar with the neck facing down.

4. Stuff the cotton balls into the neck of the bottle.

5. Put the activated charcoal into the gallon plastic bag, and use the mallet to crush it. Pour the crushed charcoal into the bottle.

6. Pour the sand into the bottle, then add the gravel to the bottle.

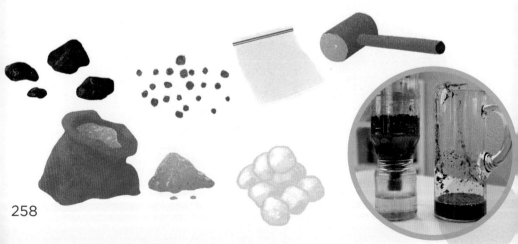

7. Loosen the cap of the bottle as far as you can, but do not remove it.

8. Slowly pour muddy water into the bottle.

9. Observe what happens as the muddy water is filtered into the mason jar.

"Dr. Fizzlebop, what's happening?"

The gravel, sand, and charcoal—which act as a filter—are removing the contaminants from the water in three stages. First, the largest particles are separated from the muddy water as they pass through the rocks. Then, smaller particles are removed as they pass through the sand. Finally, as the water passes through the activated charcoal, the smallest contaminants are removed, along with certain chemicals. The cotton balls make sure that the activated charcoal stays put in the filter. As the muddy water passes through each stage of the filtration system, it gets cleaner and cleaner.

FIZZ FACT: The water would need to go through more steps to be safe, so don't drink it.

Devotional

Watching the muddy water pour into the filter and come out a lot clearer was fizztastic, even if there was no fizz involved. Though now I'm wondering how we might incorporate fizz in the future! Filters even more sophisticated (which means advanced) than ours can remove 99.9% of all contaminants from water to make it safe to drink.

You know, the sin in our lives is kind of like this muddy water. Sin is dirty and yucky. But unlike our filter, which can get the muddy water kind of clean—or even advanced filters that can make dirty water 99.9% clean—there is something that can clean our sins away 100%. That's salvation through Jesus Christ!

Here's the deal: getting pure and clean from our sins is super-simple. First John 1:9 says, "If we confess our sins to him, he is faithful and just to forgive us our sins and to cleanse us from all wickedness."

Confess equals cleanse. It's that easy.

In the Bible, we also read about how water is used as a symbol of our cleansing from sin. Now, the actual water of baptism doesn't take away sin—it's faith in Jesus that does that. But baptism is a symbolic moment for any new Christian to show his or her desire to repent of sin and turn to God. Publicly professing your faith in God is a wondrous moment, and one you should discuss with your pastor if you haven't been baptized yet.

Every Easter Sunday at my church, people are given the opportunity to be baptized. Some people plan ahead for that weekend, while others are so stirred by the wondrous news of Jesus' death and resurrection that they get up out of their seats and walk down into the baptismal tub. And from the sidelines, as I watch people—strangers I don't even know—commit their lives to God, I can't stop myself from crying great tears of joy.

When Jesus comes into our life and we confess our sins, we throw off the dirt and mud of sin. We are washed clean, and a new day in our life begins.

Collecting Your Family's Data

Describe the contrast between the filtered water and the muddy water you poured in (color, texture, smell).

....

Pour the water through the filter a few more times. Does it continue to get clearer the more times you pour it through the filter?

....

Have you asked Jesus to cleanse you of your sins? Why or why not?

....

Prayer Time

As a family, take a moment to pray for each other. Thank God for the ways he is working in your life. And pray for those you know who still need to turn to God and follow him.

FIZZ EXTRA: **Share Your Story**

If anyone in your family has confessed their sins and chosen to follow Jesus, have them share why they made that choice and what their life has been like since. If anyone has been baptized, ask them to share about that experience and what it was like to be baptized.

HOLIDAY
BONUS ACTIVITIES

NEW YEAR'S EVE

Party Poppers
(Ecclesiastes 3:1-8)

Introduction

A giant glittering ball, fireworks, sparkling juice, counting down to midnight—there are so many fun traditions used to mark the New Year! How does your family celebrate? Growing up, it was a favorite holiday of mine, because we got to stay up until midnight and watch the ball drop in New York City. Plus, we always had a variety of wondrous appetizers. And best of all, as an exuberant young scientist, I enjoyed observing how people of different ages tried to keep themselves awake for the big countdown. My grandpa never made it past ten. Those who made it until midnight were rewarded with pulling the strings of our party poppers. Today we're going to create our very own party poppers with items you have around your house!

WARNING! This experiment requires scissors. Safety first! Do not aim confetti poppers at other humans or animals.

Fizzlebop Supply List

- Balloon
- Scissors
- Cardboard toilet paper tube
- Duct tape (colored tape adds some flair)
- Markers
- Stickers
- Colored paper
- Confetti

The Experiment

1. Without inflating your balloon, tie it closed.

2. Cut ½ inch (1.25 cm) off from the non-tied end of the balloon.

3. Stretch the newly cut opening over one end of the toilet paper tube and secure with tape.

4. Decorate your confetti popper with markers, stickers, and colored paper.

5. Pour confetti into the open end of the tube. Hold it so the balloon end faces down.

6. Count down to midnight, then pull down on the balloon end and let go. Happy New Year!

"Dr. Fizzlebop, what's happening?"

For every action there is an equal and opposite reaction—so says Newton's third law. So when you pull down on the balloon, you are storing up energy. Then when you let go, that stored energy releases upward and forces the confetti to explode out of the party popper tube. Neato!

Devotional

As the year comes to a close, I like to look back and ponder what the year held, both the good and the bad. There are always things I think I could have done better, and there are things I celebrate having done well. There are things that were out of my control, and there are things that I had to leave up to God.

Then I look forward to the year ahead. What do I want to accomplish and explore? What do I want to improve? I'm not much for New Year's resolutions (which are firm commitments to do something), but I do enjoy making a list of things that I'd like to try, improve upon, or accomplish in the next year.

Have you ever made a list of goals? If you did, what would be at the top?

I recognize that my list will change throughout the year. God will open some doors, and he may close others, even if only temporarily. In my heart I understand that God knows what is best for my life. I'll admit there are times when I fool myself into thinking I know what's best. The thing is, I have no idea what the future holds. Life changes, but God does not, and he knows what is in store for each of us.

Turn to Ecclesiastes chapter 3 in your Bible. Verse 1 tells us, "For everything there is a season, a time for every activity under heaven." Keep reading, all the way through verse 8.

These verses are a list of opposites, telling us that God has foreseen (which means already knows) everything that will happen under him. He isn't caught by surprise. He knows the right time to weep and the right time to laugh, to plant and to uproot. What matters is that we trust in him as we move through these seasons of life.

As you prepare for the New Year, don't make resolutions you can't keep. Make goals of what you'd like to do or change this year, and then give it all over to God in prayer. Trust him with your desires, and trust him to know the timing of every moment of your life.

Collecting Your Family's Data

How high did your confetti go? To the ceiling?

Does your confetti popper shoot farther with more or less confetti loaded into it? Try it both ways!

How can you make God a bigger focus in your life this year?

Think of one thing you can do to help your community or family this year.

Prayer Time

Amazing Creator, thank you for new beginnings and for the opportunity to make our lives new in you. Thank you that we can always rely on you to be with us as we experience change in our lives. Amen.

VALENTINE'S DAY

Fizzing Hearts
(1 Corinthians 13)

Introduction

Love is in the air. And for today's experiment, we're going to use something I love, which is fizz! It will also involve the world-wide symbol for love: a heart. This fizzy fun activity includes a super-simple chemical reaction and a colorful creation. And we're going to go deeper into the meaning of love and how God wants it to be at the core (which means center) of all we do. After all, he is the God of love, and we are his people.

FIZZ FACT: Did you know that this holiday was named for St. Valentine? Legend has it, he may have sent the first valentine too, writing a letter to the girl he loved and signing it, "Your Valentine."

Fizzlebop Supply List

- Paper
- School glue
- 2 tbsp (30 g) baking soda
- 1/4 cup (60 mL) vinegar
- 8-oz (240 mL) mason jar
- Red food coloring
- Baking sheet
- Eyedropper

The Experiment

1. On the piece of paper, use glue to make several heart-shaped outlines of varying sizes.

   FIZZ TIP: Make the hearts at least 2 inches (5 cm) apart.

2. Sprinkle baking soda over all the glue hearts.

   FIZZ TIP: Be sure to completely cover the glue with the baking soda.

3. Let the baking soda–covered hearts dry for 2 hours.

4. Pour the vinegar into the jar. Add 7 drops of red food coloring to the vinegar.

5. Set the paper with the hearts on your baking sheet.

6 Use the eyedropper to add several drops of vinegar to the center of each heart.

FIZZ TIP: The larger the heart, the more vinegar you may need to add.

7 Observe the wondrous fizz!

"Dr. Fizzlebop, what's happening?"

You've made a fizzing chemical reaction by adding the vinegar to the baking soda. Baking soda is a base and vinegar is an acid. When these two combine, they produce a gas called carbon dioxide. And you know what carbon dioxide is great for? Fizz, lots of fizz. So when the two react, the fizzing begins. You can hear it, see it, and even smell it.

Devotional

What does the Bible say about love? Read 1 Corinthians 13 and fill in the blanks for verses 4-7.

Love is .... and ....

Love is not .... or ....
or .... or ....

It does not ....

It is not .... ,
and it keeps no ....

It does not rejoice about ....
but rejoices whenever ....

Love never ...., never ....,
is always ...., and ....
through every circumstance.

The Bible is the most definitive (which means complete and trusted) book of knowledge, and its definition is the exact way God wants us to understand and practice his magnificent creation of love.

In fact, in verse 13, the Bible says love is the greatest of the three things that will last forever. The greatest is love.

Guess what? God loved the world he created so much that he gave his Son as a sacrifice so that we could be forgiven of our sins and live with him in heaven eternally (which means forever). It's the most fizztastic way he could show his love.

Love isn't about a box of chocolates—or fizzy hearts. It's about caring for those around us unconditionally—without jealousy, forgiving them, having faith and hope, and remaining steadfast through life's trials. It's about having patience and kindness for everyone in our lives, whether family members, friends, or strangers we have only just met.

So if you're sending any valentines today, do it with the pure love God gives to you.

Collecting Your Family's Data

Describe the reaction between the vinegar and baking soda.

....

Do you think different shapes (not hearts) would react differently?

....

What might the reaction be like if you didn't let the glue dry for 2 hours?

....

What parts of God's definition of love do you need to work on?

....

Prayer Time

Amazing Creator, you designed love, and you showed us just how much you love us when you sent your Son, Jesus Christ, to die for our sins. May we learn to practice the patience, kindness, and forgiveness that is your love. Amen.

EASTER

Fizzy Easter Egg Dyeing
(Matthew 28:1-10)

Introduction

It's going to be a fizztastic Easter here at Fizzlebop Labs! Eggs represent the beginning of new life—which is what Jesus offers through salvation—and coloring the eggs makes me think of a vibrant (which means bright) and beautiful celebration. Add in a bit of my absolute favorite thing—you guessed it, fizz!— and you have an amazing experiment along with a celebration of Jesus' resurrection.

FIZZ FACT: There are four accounts in the Bible about Jesus' resurrection. You can find them in Matthew 28, Mark 16, Luke 24, and John 20.

WARNING! This experiment can be messy, so use a washable surface.

Fizzlebop Supply List

- 1 tsp (5 mL) food coloring (use as many different colors as you want)
- 2 tbsp (30 g) baking soda per color
- 1 glass mixing bowl per color
- Spoons
- A dozen hard-boiled eggs or more
- Plate
- Wide paintbrushes
- 8-oz (240 mL) mason jars (1 per egg)
- 1/2 cup (120 mL) vinegar per egg

The Experiment

1. Mix 1 tsp (5 mL) food coloring and 2 tbsp (30 g) baking soda in a mixing bowl. Stir the mixture together. Repeat this step in different bowls for each color you wish to make.

   FIZZ TIP: If your food coloring or dye has vinegar in it, this may create a small reaction. Do not be alarmed—it will not affect the experiment.

2. Set the eggs on a plate to keep them from rolling off your work surface.

3. Paint the paste from the bowls onto the eggs with the paint-brushes.

   FIZZ TIP: The thicker the layers of paste, the better the reaction will be.

4. Fill each mason jar with ½ cup (120 mL) of vinegar. Fill 1 mason jar for each fizzy Easter egg you make.

5 Lower the eggs into the jars of vinegar, and observe the fizz-tastic and eggcellent egg dyeing!

6 Remove the eggs and enjoy. Be sure to discard your leftover vinegar.

"Dr. Fizzlebop, what's happening?"

Why does your egg fizz? The mixture you made contains baking soda. When an acid such as vinegar is added to a base (baking soda, in this case), the result is a chemical reaction that releases carbon dioxide gas. The result is fizz—lots of fizz.

Devotional

What comes to mind when you think of Easter Sunday? Eggs, candy, a bunny (furry or chocolate), a tomb, an angel, death defeated, a celebration?

When I was younger, hunting for Easter eggs and opening them to find candy was an event I looked forward to. That hasn't changed! But as I got older, I began to understand what it meant for Jesus to die on the Cross and then to look directly at death and defeat it forever. He gave sinners the chance at new life, to be reborn in the saving grace of the Cross.

I still like to think about Easter eggs when spring comes around, but not just for the candy inside. These days, Easter eggs remind me of the Resurrection.

You can read about Jesus rising from the tomb in several books of the Bible, but today I want to focus on Matthew 28:1-10. Take a moment to read this passage as a family.

I love how Matthew describes the moment of discovery, when Mary Magdalene and the other Mary learned that Jesus had risen. Here was this angel sent from God to meet the two women. He glowed with all the brilliance of one who represents heaven, yet after rolling away this massive stone, he hopped up and sat down. The guards fainted, but not the two followers of Jesus.

After hearing the angel's message, the two women rushed away to share it with the disciples. Jesus met them and greeted them, and they ran to him, grasped his feet, and worshiped him.

Can you imagine? Can you see it? You're running down a dusty road, having just seen an angel, having just learned that Jesus conquered death, and then there he is walking toward you! You can touch him and hear him. The Son of God has risen!

If any doubt remained after the angel said Jesus had risen, it would vanish once he was standing before you. There is no way you could not believe 100% that this was the Messiah. As I read the accounts of Jesus in the Bible—and about the multitude of people who saw and interacted with him both before and after his death—I have no doubt that Jesus is indeed the Son of God, sent to earth to rescue you and me.

So that is why I zealously celebrate Easter with passion and joy and exuberance. The magnificent King of kings has wondrously risen!

Collecting Your Family's Data

What happened when you added the baking soda–coated eggs to the vinegar? Describe the reaction (sight, sound, smell).

....

What is your favorite Easter tradition?

....

How might you have reacted if you met Jesus on the road after he rose from the dead?

....

Prayer Time

Magnificent Son, thank you for coming to this earth with the mission of saving us. May we always remember what you did on Easter and celebrate with joy and passion. Amen.

THANKSGIVING

Squishy Turkeys
(Psalm 107:8-9)

Introduction

Greetings! I am thankful that you have joined me today at Fizzlebop Labs. In fact, I'm feeling *besonders dankbar* (which means "extra thankful" in German). Our experiment is quite fun, and I think it'll have you giggling a bit when you're done. Be sure to have everyone participate and make their very own squishy turkey.

WARNING! This experiment requires borax. Safety first! Do not ingest borax.

Fizzlebop Supply List

- Nitrile exam glove
- Tall glass
- 1/2 cup (120 mL) white glue
- 1 cup (240 mL) water
- Measuring cup (1 cup or 240 mL)
- 1 tsp (5 g) borax powder
- Colorful markers

The Experiment

1. Put the glove fingers down in a tall glass, and stretch the opening of the glove over the rim of the glass.

2. Pour the glue into the glove.

3. Pour ½ cup (120 mL) of the water into the glove.

4. Take the glove out of the glass, hold the glove closed, and carefully squish it to mix the contents.

5. In a separate measuring cup, mix the borax with another ½ cup (120 mL) water. Pour the water and borax mixture into the glove.

6. Knot the glove like a balloon, then squish the glove to mix all the ingredients.
   FIZZ TIP: Do not squish the glove too hard.

7. Decorate your squishy turkey with markers.

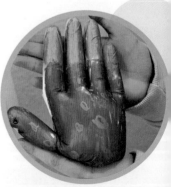

"Dr. Fizzlebop, what's happening?"

In this experiment, two of the ingredients—glue and borax—mix together to form long chains of molecules. These chains are called polymers. The water allows these polymers to move around inside the glove. When they do, they stretch and stick together.

Devotional

Thanksgiving is a time of reflection and a time to be grateful for what God has done. In my family we have a tradition on Thanksgiving. Before we eat dinner, we go around the room and share what we are thankful for. Let me tell you, we have a big extended family that celebrates Thanksgiving together, so when I was a kid, this time of sharing seemed to last for weeks . . . especially because the dessert table with all my favorites was set up in the same room, including my mom's apple pie (I was never a big pumpkin pie fan)! But as I grew, I began to truly appreciate this time of reflection. As I listened to what my uncle, or cousin, or grandma were thankful for that year, I was filled with gratefulness for the many, many things God was always doing in the lives of the people I love.

And that was just my family! Imagine what God is doing every second of every day all around the world for the billions of people who live here on earth. The world should be bursting with thankfulness and happiness. Psalm 107:8-9 says, "Let them praise the LORD for his great love and for the wonderful things he has done for them. For he satisfies the thirsty and fills the hungry with good things."

In the Bible, we also read, "Rejoice always, pray continually, give thanks in all circumstances; for this is God's will for you in Christ Jesus" (1 Thessalonians 5:16-18, NIV). "All circumstances" doesn't only mean when life is fizztastic—it means even when life is arduous (which means difficult). These are the times when we should turn our eyes and hearts to God and pray. These are the times we must go deeper into his arms of hope, love, and joy.

FIZZ FACT: Thanksgiving holidays are celebrated all around the world, though they're not all on the same day. In Germany, the holiday is called Erntedankfest, and in the United Kingdom, it's known as the Harvest Festival.

Collecting Your Family's Data

Describe the feeling of the glue-borax turkey when you squish it between your hands.

....

What do you think it would feel like if you had only filled the glove with water?

....

THANKFULNESS LIST

As a family, come up with twelve things you are thankful for. They can be from the past year or anytime during your life.

....

....

....

....

....

....

....

....

....

....

....

Share why you're thankful for each of these things.

Prayer Time

As a family, use your list of thankfulness to give thanks to God and reflect on what he has done for you.

FIZZ EXTRA: Turkeylicious Creativity Contest

Make it a competition! Have everyone vote on whose turkey is best decorated. The winner and runner-up get to break the wishbone this Thanksgiving.

CHRISTMAS

Fizzing Christmas Trees
(The Story of St. Nicholas)

Introduction

Christmas! I don't know about your family, but on December 1 we're ready to get in the Christmas spirit. We start our Advent calendar of 25 days of family activities and it's full of family fun. We ring the bell for the Salvation Army, ice-skate as a family, put on our own Christmas play, and so much more. Christmas can be such a wondrous time of family and giving. And today we're going to have a fizztastic experiment that will truly fizz and fizz and fizz.

FIZZ TIP: You can download the Fizzlebop family's 25 Days of Advent activity calendar at Fizzlebop.com.

WARNING! This experiment requires scissors. Safety first!

Fizzlebop Supply List

- Large glass mixing bowl
- Spoon
- 2 cups (450 g) baking soda (plus a little extra for sprinkling)
- 1/2 cup (120 mL) water
- Green food coloring
- Sequins and glitter
- Paper plate
- Scissors
- Tape
- Tray (that can go in the freezer)
- 1 tbsp (15 mL) vinegar
- Eyedropper

The Experiment

1. Pour the baking soda into the mixing bowl. Slowly add the water and 3 drops of green food coloring.

   FIZZ TIP: This mixture should create a crumbly but packable dough.

2. Stir sequins and glitter into the mixture.

3. Cut a paper plate in half. Then wrap it into a cone and fasten it with tape. (Use the other half for a second fizztastic tree!)

4. Flip the cone upside down. Tightly pack the dough into the cone shape.

   FIZZ TIP: Make sure the dough is tightly packed all the way to the tip.

5. Place the cone of dough in the freezer on a tray. Let it sit overnight.

6 The next day, peel off the paper cone and set your "tree" back on the tray.

7 Add a light snowfall of baking soda around the bottom for more fizzing action.

8 Mix the vinegar with 3 drops of green food coloring.

9 Use the eyedropper to squirt a few drops of green vinegar on top of your Christmas tree. Observe what you see.

0 Continue dripping vinegar on the tree until all the fizztastic fun is over.

"Dr. Fizzlebop, what's happening?"

You made a fizzing Christmas chemical reaction by adding the vinegar to the molded baking-soda tree. Baking soda is a base, and vinegar is an acid. When these two combine, they produce a gas called carbon dioxide. And you know what carbon dioxide is great for? Fizz, lots of fizz! So when the two react, the fizzing begins. You can hear it, see it, and even smell it.

Devotional

You probably have many wondrous Christmas traditions. At the Fizzlebop home, we exuberantly celebrate Advent with various activities, we open special pajamas on Christmas Eve, we make fizzy Christmas trees like you just did, and we celebrate Jesus' birthday with a birthday cake! We also have a tradition called St. Nicking, where we leave gifts anonymously (which means secretly) on the doorstep of someone who needs a little extra at Christmas.

Have you ever heard of a man named St. Nicholas, also known as St. Nick? St. Nick lived a long time ago (around

AD 280) in a place called Asia Minor, which is part of modern-day Turkey (the country, not the bird). As a boy, he traveled widely with his parents and saw many magnificent things, but sadly both of his parents died in an epidemic (which is an outbreak of sickness), leaving him an orphan. Nicholas inherited his parents' fortune, and as a strong Christian, he lived out Jesus' teachings on generosity.

We can learn what Jesus had to say about being generous in the story of the Rich Young Ruler (Mark 10:17-31). Have you read that part of the Bible? If not, turn there now and check it out!

Jesus told the rich young man, "Go and sell all your possessions and give the money to the poor, and you will have treasure in heaven. Then come, follow me."

What the young rich man found to be a huge obstacle, Nicholas followed with all his heart. He gave generously from his inheritance and often gave anonymously. Not only did Nicholas want to give as Jesus had commanded, but he didn't want to be praised or glorified by doing so. He knew that all he had came from God, and therefore it wasn't really his at all.

To me, St. Nick is such a marvelous example of what Christmas is all about. When God gave us his Son, he gave the greatest gift he could. Jesus gave his life so people could be saved. It's a free gift for anyone who chooses to follow him. Can you see how St. Nick's selfless giving pointed toward what God and his Son, Jesus, both gave freely?

This Christmas, consider how you can give generously and anonymously to someone who needs to feel God's exuberant, overwhelming love. I promise you'll feel fizztastic inside, because when we do what God asks, we are filled with wondrous joy.

Collecting Your Family's Data

Describe your dough Christmas tree when you removed it from the paper-plate mold.

Describe what happened to the tree when you added the vinegar.

....

What traditions does your family have at Christmas? Are there any new traditions you'd like to start this year?

....

What is a way you can celebrate Jesus' birthday by showing his love to someone in your community?

....

Prayer Time

As a family, pray for friends, family members, and people in your community who might need a little extra support this year. Ask God to reveal needs to you throughout the Christmas season.

FIZZ EXTRA: St. Nicking at Night

The Fizzlebop family has many Christmas traditions, and we want to share them with you. One of our favorites is exploring and acting out the story of St. Nick. Take on this FIZZ EXTRA and show Christmas spirit to someone in your community this year.

Plus read Dr. Fizzlebop's list of 25 Advent ideas and activities.

Find the ST. NICKING AT NIGHT activity at Fizzlebop.com, or scan this QR Code and click or tap FIZZ EXTRA.

Glossary

Absorbent—able to soak up energy or liquid

Acid—a chemical substance that can neutralize or dissolve some substances

Air resistance—a force caused by air as an object moves through it; also known as drag

Amorphous—not having a definite form

Amplify—to expand or increase

Atom—smallest particle of an element; composed of protons, neutrons, and electrons

Base—compound that can neutralize an acid or react with an acid to form a salt

Boil—to raise the temperature of a liquid until it begins to bubble and generates vapor

Brittle—stiff enough to break rather than bend

Carbon dioxide—the gas you breathe out, and the same one that makes soda fizztastically fizzy

Centripetal force—a force directed toward the center of rotation; required to keep objects moving in a curved path

Chemical reaction—a change that occurs between two or more chemicals; results in a new substance

Chlorophyll—a green pigment that helps plants absorb energy from light

Compression—pressing or flattening something

Crystal—solid substance with a regularly repeating geometric form

Density—mass in each unit of volume: the higher the mass in an area, the higher the density

Dissolve—to mix a substance into a liquid, creating a solution

Electron—a negatively charged particle in an atom

Endothermic process—a process in which an object borrows heat from objects around it

Erosion—the reduction of something by outside force

Evaporation—the conversion of liquid to vapor

Expand—to get bigger

Ferrous—containing iron

Fluctuation—a change

Friction—the force that causes two surfaces to resist moving against one another

Geode—a small cavity in a rock lined with crystals or other mineral matter

Germination—when a plant begins to sprout

Levitate—to float in the air

Magnitude—size

Minuscule—tiny

Moldable—able to be formed into a shape

Molecule—the smallest particle of a compound or substance; made up of one or more atoms

Neutron—a neutral particle in an atom

Observe—to watch carefully

Oxidize—to combine something with oxygen

Organic—living matter or something related to living matter

Ovoid—an egg-shaped object

Payload—an object being carried or transported

Phototropism—the growth of a plant as a response to light

Proton—a positively charged particle in an atom

Replicate—to copy; duplicate

Saturated—the state of a solution when it can't absorb anything more

Soda—a beverage also known as pop

Solution—the mixture formed when one substance is combined with another

Static electricity—a stationary electric charge that builds up on the surface of an object until it can be released

Supersaturation—the state of a solution when it contains more of a substance than required for saturation

Surfactant—a substance that reduces the surface tension between two liquids

Taut—tight; tense

Transparent—the quality of being see-through or clear

Vibration—particles quickly moving up and down or back and forth as a result of equilibrium being disturbed

Vortex—air or liquid swirling in a circular motion, pulling matter toward it

Acknowledgments

Amazing Creator, thank you for the world you've intricately designed. You thought of everything from the sun and the moon, to magnificent rainbows, to plants making oxygen from carbon dioxide so I can breathe, to who I am and who I am becoming.

To my wife, Ashley, who always encourages me to keep creating and pursuing my ideas. You believe in me and help me stay focused. And also thanks for that fizzilicious Super-Simple Triple Chocolate Chunk Caramel Cookies recipe. YUM!

Kinley, Elsie, Waverly, Declan, you've put so much into this book. Thank you for helping me with every experiment and smiling for the camera and changing clothes for the zillionth time. This book would not be possible without each of you. You make me the proudest daddy in the world.

Linda, you gave Dr. Fizzlebop life. Thank you for always listening to my ideas and encouraging me to keep at it. Asking me to host Summer Camp meant so much and truly brought Dr. Fizzlebop into existence. Your friendship means the world.

Jackie, how grateful I am for your masterful mind on this project. Designing this book on a speedy timeline and with so much imagery was a Herculean task, and you did it stupendously. Alyssa and Danika, thanks for molding my words and ideas into this wondrous book and helping Dr. Fizzlebop get his thoughts across more precisely. You helped Dr. Fizzlebop find his voice with every edit and suggestion. Kristi the marketing extraordinaire, I've met someone who is more excited about marketing than I am, and I am thrilled. And Mike and Ian, you prepared a whole lot of Fizzy Oranges and sold the book before it could be sold—thank you! Christine, thank you—without the dotted i's and crossed t's, there'd be no Fizzlebop. Madeline, we perhaps set the record for earliest-ever PR interview for a book that can't even be ordered yet, woohoo! Debbie, thank you for all your marvelous dedication to the details—the book will fizz even more now. Kathy and Donna, thank you for experimenting to ensure fizztastic results for families. Lisanne, consistency is critical to stupendous science fun, so thank you. Babette, keep those promotional ideas coming! Because of each of you, many families and kids around God's amazing world will grow closer to him, knowing that he is the one who designed it all.

Steve, thanks for helping me forge ahead on this crazy path as an author. No matter what I throw at you—picture books, devotionals, middle-grade fiction—you always know what to do.

Sean, Shaun, Chris, Joanna, thank you for helping to bring Dr. Fizzlebop across the deadline and pouring your thoughts and creativity into this book.

Mr. Bill, I probably wasn't the student you expected to write a science book, but it never stopped you from encouraging and teaching me. And here, after all this time, you're still cheering me on and helping me with my homework.

Mom and Dad, as always your encouragement of me from the beginning to forever gives me the foundation to feel free to create and take chances.

Thank you, Byington, Breg, Lutz, and Thomas families—your feedback on the Fizzlebop experiments was super helpful in making it more awesome for families all over the world. And thank you, Kaitlana and Kyler O'Neil and the Hasley family, for your generous donation to the Fizzlebop Labs web series production. Because of you, I'll be able to provide fizztastic videos of the experiments for all to see.

And to you the reader, thank you for picking up this book and joining Dr. Fizzlebop in the lab. I truly hope you'll have as much fizztastic fun doing these experiments and devotions as I did. And I hope your family grows closer together, laughs a whole lot, and deepens their faith and understanding of our Amazing Creator.

About the Author

Brock Eastman, Dr. Fizzlebop's alter ego, is passionate about marketing and storytelling. His desire to show kids how faith and science connect is the driving force behind his Dr. Fizzlebop persona. He writes feature stories and the Dr. Fizzlebop column for *Clubhouse* and *Clubhouse Jr.* magazines. He hosts Tyndale Kids' Virtual Summer Camp and the Fizzlebop Labs online video series, as well as cohosting the Story Biz podcast. Besides creating a crazy, fun science devotional, Brock has written and sold over 150,000 copies of several books and series including the Quest for Truth series, *Daddy's Favorite Sound, Mommy's Favorite Smell, Bedtime on Noah's Ark*, the Sages of Darkness series, and *Showdown with the Shepherd* from the Imagination Station series. He currently resides in Colorado and loves cooking, doing puzzles with his wonderful wife, and reading stories to his four fizztastic kids each night.

FOR ADVENTURERS

The Wormling series

Red Rock Mysteries series

FOR COMEDIANS

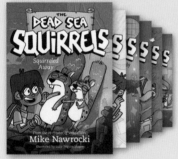

The Dead Sea Squirrels series

FOR ARTISTS

Made to Create with All My
Heart and Soul

Be Bold

FOR ANIMAL LOVERS

Winnie the Horse Gentler series

Starlight Animal Rescue series

CP1337